Since 2003, Jude Rogers has written about arts and culture for the *Guardian*, *Observer*, *Sunday Times*, *Times Saturday Review*, *Daily Telegraph*, *New Statesman*, *The Word*, *MOJO*, *Q*, *NME*, The Quietus, *Wire* and *The Gentlewoman*. She has made acclaimed documentaries for Radio 4, including the 2021 series *A Life in Music*, and presents the White Rabbit music books podcast, Songbook. She has interviewed artists from Paul McCartney to Dolly Parton, Damon Albarn to Billie Eilish, Laurie Anderson to Michael Stipe, Debbie Harry to the Pet Shop Boys.

The Sound of Being Human

How Music Shapes Our Lives

Jude Rogers

WHITE RABBIT

First published in Great Britain in 2022 by White Rabbit
This paperback edition published in 2023 by White Rabbit
an imprint of The Orion Publishing Group Ltd
Carmelite House, 50 Victoria Embankment
London EC4Y 0DZ

An Hachette UK Company

1 3 5 7 9 10 8 6 4 2

A CIP catalogue record for this book is
available from the British Library.

ISBN (Mass Market Paperback) 978 1 4746 2294 3
ISBN (eBook) 978 1 4746 1505 1
ISBN (Audio) 978 1 4746 1506 8

Typeset by Born Group
Printed and bound in Great Britain by Clays Ltd, Elcograf S.p.A.

MIX
Paper from
responsible sources
FSC® C104740

www.whiterabbitbooks.co.uk
www.orionbooks.co.uk

For my Dad,
and for little me

Contents

TRACK LISTING

Before the Music Starts

Press <PLAY> to play the recording for the first time.
Press <PLAY> again during playback to pause.

When I think about where music can take us, how music can affect us and shape us, this is where I travel.

An open front door on a cold Monday morning. A man is standing just over the threshold, preparing to go. The porch framing him is a soft winter grey. The terrazzo tiles at his feet are glittering like jewels. The bushes beyond him are getting ready for spring when they will come alive with fuchsias.

The man's face is gentle under sleepy-wide, dark brown eyes. He has a heavy moustache, as many young men do in South Wales in 1984. His hair is glossy-thick, shiny-blue-black, the hair of a Celt over cow-like lashes. His familiar smile is forcing itself up at the corners. His body is at odds with it, bent over two walking sticks, mismatching.

A little girl is standing on the doormat. She has a blunt fringe, doughy cheeks, pudgy hands. She is wearing patent T-bar shoes and her school uniform. There is something she has to do while the man is away, on her own. He has asked her to do it: she has to find out something, and tell him about it when he returns.

She is thinking about it as she stands on the doormat, looking up at him. Five days apart stretch ahead for them. Five days for him to get fixed, to get better.

I love you, he says. I'll see you on Friday.

My father holds my little chin in his hand.

And then he says the thing that has stayed with me for the rest of my life: 'Let me know who gets to number one.'

*

Dad died two days later. He was thirty-three. I was five. He went into hospital on the Monday for an operation to ease his ankylosing spondylitis, the condition that was causing his body to curve, twist and bend. At hospital, he would get a shiny new hip. Once he came out, he would be able to walk more easily, play with me and my baby brother, Jon.

Dad also loved pop music. I loved pop music. In those days, the Top 40 came out on a Tuesday. Dad's operation was on the Wednesday. He would be home by the Friday.

I don't remember how or when I found out what song had got to number one. That detail is awkwardly cut out of my memory, like it's been lopped out by a child let loose with pinking shears. I do remember how excited I felt to find out the answer, because it was 'Pipes of Peace' by Paul McCartney, a song about giving things to little children so they could learn, about lighting a candle to love.

As I got older, I'd look at vinyl albums of Dad's in the old storage cube under our hi-fi, their spines outwards, many of them faded and fraying. I remember finding McCartney's solo debut album from 1970, running my thumb over the cherries on the front of its sleeve. On the back cover was his baby daughter Mary, inside his warm jacket, being looked after.

Dad went under the anaesthetic on the morning of 11 January 1984. Blood stopped travelling to his brain and it never travelled again.

When I go back to the morning I was last with him, to those cow-like lashes, the porch, the tiles, the hibernating flowers, the thing that stands out more than anything is his request to know something about a song. Since I've become older than my father ever was, in the last ten years, I've started to ask myself why this detail arrives first, before everything. Why did the identification of a set of verses and choruses matter so much? Why has it carried such a weight in my mind?

I used to think I was just being nostalgic for a sweet, geeky connection between father and daughter. Dad was trusting me to find out a statistic, like a football score, perhaps. But over time, I realised there was something deeper going on. Dad and I weren't rooting for players to score goals. We were rooting for players who had come together in the studio in the service of a song – something stitched together from wisps of melodies, harmonies and rhythms, something that also, enchantingly, stitched *us* together. We were rooting for the two of us to be people for whom songs were extensions of their ordinary lives.

As I got older, I realised there was another dynamic pulsing away in the murk of my memories. Thirty years after my father died, I became a mother. Since my son was a toddler, I have noticed him responding to music, catching my breath as his cow-like lashes licked up, followed by the corners of his smile. A pattern was repeating itself in these movements, like a beloved old recording once again revolving. Music, I now knew beyond measure, was a truly remarkable thing.

This realisation had me tunnelling back to songs that exploded like supernovas in the early years of my childhood, and others that tumbled me through my adolescence. I then arrived at songs that carried me through adulthood in moments of desire, despair, recovery and resolution; songs that still keep me stimulated, soothed, alert, afloat.

I started thinking about what a song is as a historical object and a mercurial carrier of multiple meanings. I also thought about how and why we use songs as people. A song can be a means of seduction as well as a sedative, a dagger to the heart, a buoy, an escape hatch. It is something we can turn on and off, but it can also catch us by surprise. A song has a consciousness, almost, a life of its own.

When I was a little girl, especially in the dense, deadening cloud of my loss, I didn't realise how much of my life would be structured around songs, both personally and professionally. I've been writing about songs now as a journalist for nearly two decades, and had many conversations with people who write, perform and record them; people whose songs were mine and mine alone through the end of one century and the beginning of another, and people who my dad would have remembered. Elton John, Chrissie Hynde, Robert Plant and Marianne Faithfull are people who come to mind straightaway. There are many others he might have known, on black vinyl or brown tape, in his thirty-three years.

I've spent mornings in cafes and offices with artists who filled my childhood with colour; afternoons in studios and stadiums with musicians who helped me make new friends in school and university; nights backstage and in bars with new idols I first adored as a grown-up. I've tried to keep my ears open, my mind spinning through the years like a seven-inch, a C90, a CD. I have carried Dad with me through my encounters, imagining the conversations I could have had with him afterwards, thinking about how much a father and daughter could have shared but didn't share.

He always looks like he did in the porch when I think of him, leaning over on his walking sticks, his eyes full of love, me looking into them for acceptance. When I think of him there, I also think about how he trusted me to tell him a story about a song. It still breaks my heart that I couldn't stick to that promise. So in this book, I finally do what I meant to do, from the vantage point of a woman who has long grown up: I tell him the story that I was going to tell him after he came home, the story that was going to bond us even more tightly. I also share with him other stories that have come since he's gone, and let him know about the person I became.

But this is not just a book about my father. It is not even a book just about me. It is a book about music told through the lens of a life. It is a book about how songs can fundamentally shape the identities of people who respond to them and fully embrace them; it is also a book about why music holds so much power for people.

The rhythms of certain questions about music have become more consistent and persistent for me as I've got older. How do songs affect our emotions so profoundly? How can they activate memories instantly? How exactly do they tie us to other people? Why do people react emotionally when musicians die? How do they make us want to dance, just like that, when a familiar riff suddenly kinks out of the speakers and swirls around a room in a club or in a kitchen or a supermarket aisle? Why do small collections of sounds, arranged by a particular set of people at a particular place and time, seem to galvanise our limbs and smiles, our relationships and occupations, our external and internal lives?

To answer some of the questions, I've taken tentative steps into the worlds of the neuroscience, psychology, anthropology and sociology of music, speaking to people who know much more about these subjects than I do. I've also read piles of books, digested academic papers and absorbed documentaries, films, radio programmes and podcasts, keeping my eyes and ears open for stories about music that could help illuminate mine. Some nuggets have involved digging and dogged enquiry; others have drifted into my life accidentally, in passing, as songs often do. My motivation throughout this process has been to be an enthusiastic explorer, to cast different degrees of illumination on music's many mysteries, to link them together to create new paths of light.

This is why you'll find neuroscientists in these pages obsessed with the connections between music and memory and psychologists who understand what musicians represent as role models. You'll find experts in fandom who have been obsessives themselves and music-loving medics who understand the importance of songs at crucial life stages. You'll find music writers who were around when the songs I loved were being made, and sometimes the musicians themselves. People close to me with whom I've shared songs, who have their own stories to tell are here too, who know in their individual ways just how much music means.

I also have my own story, which I've chosen to tell through twelve significant songs from my life. Some are well-known and not particularly cool (not that I have any truck with the grisly concept of the guilty pleasure). My more obscure choices are not here for brownie points, but because they are personal favourites. I don't write expecting the reader to be an expert in any or all of them, but I hope you are encouraged to listen to these songs and linger in them, or to use them as jumping-off points to start new musical adventures.

My story includes chart pop, rap, folk, alternative rock, electronic music, reggae, Motown, Northern Soul, tender ballads and club bangers. (It is not a definitive list of my favourite songs either; I'm still despairing at the many left sitting on the cutting-room floor.) But it begins at a front door then it travels: through school changing rooms, playgrounds, teenage bedrooms, rented flats, register offices, birthing suites, recording studios, concert venues, festival fields, motorways, laybys, hospitals, memorials. It journeys widely, from Swansea to Stockholm, Düsseldorf to Detroit, Twickenham to Kingston Town, moving from euphoric communal experiences to intimate, private, personal ones.

And to tell the story properly, I've got to go back to the moment when a song first sparked a glowing light in my life, three years before that moment at the front door, to a world in which my father once walked, breathed and listened.

And while I will be writing this story for you and for me, I can't deny it: I will be carrying a memory with me, one which runs to a much-remembered melody and rhythm.

I love you.

I won't see you on Friday.

But I love you.

You're still my number one.

Track 1

Super Trouper – ABBA

How Music Beats Within Us from the Beginning

Long before my father, the sleeping fuchsias, the open front door, I find myself a tinier girl, and my first memory appears, which is of a song. I am standing at the sink in Grandma Eirwen and Grandpa Con's kitchen, my short, chubby legs on the steps of a white painted stool, right next to the back door. I say kitchen: it's a scullery tacked onto a living room in the village of Loughor, a sprawl of detached and semi-detached houses and new-build estates which grew out of a core of small steelworks and collieries.

At the southwest of the village, a muddy, lazy estuary heads out to the sea, separating us from the north coast of the Gower peninsula. Above the water sits a tiny tumble-down Norman castle, built within the earthworks of an old roman fort.

That is the past, though. This is the present. I am 'making records' in the washing-up bowl. 'Making records' was a game I invented and played a lot in my very early years. I'd start by squeezing paint from a bottle into a deep plastic tub in the sink. Grandma would then pour water in from the wonky tap, and I'd stir the colours round and round with a long, wooden spoon. Then I'd stop, lean back, watch the circles spin. I'd always watch the circles spin while I sang.

The frame around this scene is emerging, as I think of it, in rich early eighties detail. Next to me is Grandma's bottle of Amami setting lotion which she used to set her hair after washing it here, under rivulets of warm water. The Amami was bright blue, her hair bright white, like a soft bubble of launderette soap. There is a rusty old tin of Grandpa's nearby, its wrapper long wetted and scrubbed away, holding odd knives and forks and other assorted utensils. More rusty tins live in the shed just beyond the back door, past the outside toilet and the coalhouse, under a roof of downward-sloping corrugated iron, onto which my little brother and I would throw balls after school to entertain ourselves, letting them roll back into our arms.

Grandpa's British Steel overalls hang on the back of the shed door. I remember the shed feeling chaotic and forlorn; I preferred the comfort of the kitchen, the cupboards full of packet sauces and little tins opened with keys, the whirring drone of the twin tub washing machine.

Another sound would accompany this whirr, travelling into the kitchen from the living room: pop music, playing on my grandpa's big boxy radiogram. He'd bought it with his pay from Felindre Works near Swansea, where he'd worked since 1954, back when pop music was in its infancy. A fortune teller at a fair in Porthcawl had asked Grandpa for silver in her palm and told him that he'd be getting a job in the West. He became a tinning line operator, forced into early retirement after the 1980 steel strike. He hated every minute of his working life. 'Do something you like when you grow up, bach,' he said to me when I was a teenager, 'and bugger the rest.'

But in his last years of work, as the early years of my life came to be, Grandpa would come home and play music on his radiogram by Matt Monro, Johnny Mathis, Harry Belafonte, and less glamorously but still as loudly, Max Boyce, who'd sing songs from South Wales: rugby songs, drinking songs, traditional songs, rough-and-ready in their delivery, and tender versions of hymns. When the turntable wasn't going, Grandpa would play tapes, or put the radio on. The song travelling through to the kitchen on the day of my very first memory was a song being played by a DJ, wandering into our weekday routines via medium wave.

In my mind, I see my grandma, a strong alto in chapel and the village choir, singing along to it in her housecoat with a washing-up cloth in her hand. She enjoys helping me along. It's an easy song to sing along to. The chorus is in two halves, with each pivoting around a simple rhyme: 'sun' and 'one', then 'do' and 'you'. I see circles of painted water spinning quickly as we sing.

Whenever I hear ABBA's 'Super Trouper' now, there is still something in the movement in the song that feels full of sweet, genuine, unquenchable life. That sensation begins in the opening harmonies between Agnetha Fältskog and Anni-Frid Lyngstad, their voices glistening together in the reverb, then continues in the song's strolling, summery bassline and the circular movements of melody. Agnetha and Anni-Frid's voices move in sync through the verses, two fireflies flaming, but there is also a delicacy in their delivery, and a hunger for something else bristling underneath. For hope, perhaps, or the recognition and the resolution of a feeling.

*

It would be years until I knew what ABBA's 'Super Trouper' was actually about. I would encounter it regularly through my life: on daytime radio, in shops, on TV; at wedding discos in rah-rah skirts, strappy satin shift dresses, polka-dotted A-line skirts and vintage jumpsuits. I would dismiss it with a rueful shake of my head through a period of unwise pop denial in my mid-teens. By my early twenties, I had seen the error of my ways, and become a devoted, salivating fan of the song once again, as well as the band.

But my fandom now had new textures to it, as I realised 'Super Trouper' had changed. This song about a person longing for someone else was being performed by a group that was privately falling apart. By 1980, when the single came out, both couples in the band – Björn Ulvaeus and Agnetha, and Benny Andersson and Anni-Frid – had broken up. (Björn married someone else just after it was released, in fact: the music journalist, Lena Källersjö.) As an adult, I understood that lyrics didn't have to be personal, but it became clear that ABBA's biographies sharpened the edges of their later productions. These elements are more obvious in a ballad like 'The Winner Takes It All' when Agnetha is singing tough, unsparing lyrics about a break-up, put into her mouth by her ex-husband (an act I've always thought was both clever and cruel). They're subtler in songs like 1977's 'Knowing Me, Knowing You', written when the couples were still together. The production in that track layers glitter and sparkle over sad details in its lyrics, as a woman walks through an empty house, taking in familiar rooms in which children used to play.

Super Trouper was also the name of a brand of popular stage spotlight in those disco-dazzled days. A pop star should shine under its gleam, but the glare could also hit them or blind them like an ultraviolet nuclear flash. The song around it is about being lonely on an epic scale, alone in full-beam, before it starts to soothe – because someone is coming along, the lyrics say, to make things better.

Whenever I hear 'Super Trouper' today, I am inevitably far away from that kitchen where I first heard it. My grandfather died a few rooms away in his sleep, in a bed set up downstairs, just over twenty years later. My grandmother followed him eight years after that, in a hospital five miles up the road. The house was sold. The radiogram went in the house clearance. It finished its days at the bottom of the stairs like an ornament, then in the back bedroom covered up with a blanket. I like to think of the songs it once played like ghosts, softly murmuring shadows, in its internal mechanics.

Whenever I hear 'Super Trouper' now, I hear the wistfulness of passing time sew itself tighter into every syllable, every shivering sound. But I never feel lonely. I am always back in that house, in that kitchen, my hands being warmed by the sink water, my spoon stirring wildly, the twin tub purring along its soft, cyclical percussion, the ephemera of my grandparents' lives all around me. A song laces the specifics of this picture together, carries its elements along.

I have dug deep into this memory like a detective over the years, to find out when it happened and if it happened, to pin down its accuracy, its essential truth. The biggest clue is that I remember Grandma finding a line in the song funny, where the singer feels like a number one, because the song *was* number one. She would repeat this observation, as a memory, in later years; when I went round after school, where we'd play gin rummy or snap and drink milky tea, or when I'd pop home when I'd grown up, to a table still groaning with Welsh cakes and ham sandwiches, the kitchen extended and new bathroom adapted, a fancy new washing machine sitting in contemplative silence. I also found out 'Super Trouper' had been number one in October and November 1980. I was two-and-a-half on that stool, spinning soggy, paint-splattered grooves.

Not long after I became a mother, my brother Jon brought the stool up to my house in London, having saved it in the house clearance after Grandma died. The idea was that my little boy could use it too, when he was big enough. And so he did, to wash his hands, but I couldn't quite get it together to teach him to make records. The stool took me back to a time I wanted to keep to myself.

*

In October 2013, I read a newspaper article which claimed that there was finally evidence that babies could remember music they heard in the womb. This had been proved by scientists at the University of Helsinki's cognitive brain research unit, who had signed up twenty-four women for a study, all of them in their final trimester of pregnancy. Half the women were asked to play a version of 'Twinkle Twinkle Little Star' on CD to their foetuses for five days every week, at a loud volume. After the babies were born, they were told to destroy the disc. The other 50 per cent – the control group – went on with their lives without playing the song on repeat, without thinking about things up above the world so high.

Immediately after the babies were born, and then at four months, the scientists played the nursery rhyme to both groups. As the babies listened, the activity of their brain cells was measured. This involved the process of electroencephalography, which records patterns of electrical activity on the surface layer of the brain, and requires electrodes to be placed, very carefully, on the babies' delicate heads.

In each of the sittings, the babies were played the original version of the song chosen by the scientists, plus another in which a few notes were slightly altered. On every occasion, the twelve babies played the song in utero had heightened electrical activity when they heard the correct version. Crucially, the babies in the other group did not.

Project researcher Eino Partanen was, unsurprisingly, pleased. 'These results show that babies are capable of learning at a very young age, and that the effects of the learning remain apparent in the brain for a long time.' The project's principal investigator, Dr Minna Huotilainen, added that this was the first study to track how long foetal memories remain in the brain. 'The results are significant, as studying the responses in the brain let us focus on the foundations of foetal memory . . . [especially as] the early mechanisms of memory are currently unknown.'

I loved how these neuroscientists had settled on music as their implement, although I didn't know, technically, why it was a good tool. Around the same time, a camera crew filmed me at home for a BBC TV documentary about ABBA. I deliberately wore a tight top of electric blue, like the cover of their 1979 album *Voulez-Vous*. I was also twenty weeks pregnant. I liked the idea of music being around my child, working its way through my skin, sinews and muscle.

I became more interested in how music had moved me as far back as I could remember, so I began to read books that might help me understand why. I began with *This Is Your Brain on Music* by Daniel Levitin, published in 2006. Levitin was a cognitive psychologist who had only pursued this subject of study, like the far less qualified me, in his thirties. Before then, he'd helped produce albums by Steely Dan and been CEO of a San Francisco punk rock and new wave record label. Better still, he'd worked on the sound for Chris Isaak's 'Wicked Game', a song that had curled into my spine and my belly and the ends of my fingers and toes when I was twelve, igniting responses that I couldn't yet quite fathom.

Levitin wrote like a fan. He had strong opinions about the importance of music in our lives – a view that had been dismissed by other famous scientists. At the outset of his book, he recalled attending a lecture by Steven Pinker in 1997, the same year that Pinker published his landmark popular psychology book, *How the Mind Works*. 'Music is auditory cheesecake,' Pinker had written there. 'It just happens to tickle several important parts of the brain in a highly pleasurable way, as cheesecake tickles the palate.' The concept of 'auditory cheesecake' stuck in the research community's craw, Levitin explained, especially with academics who felt in their gut (and research logs) that music shouldn't be described in this way. They wanted to identify something deeper, something more fundamental, going on when we interacted with songs.

But there wasn't, insisted Pinker. Music simply pushed buttons in the auditory cortex, the part of the brain that responds to all human sounds, including those that confer emotional signals, like crying or laughing. He didn't think music could affect our ability to reproduce or survive as a species. Levitin disagreed: he thought that Pinker had missed something very important. 'If music is a non-adaptive pleasure-seeking behaviour – the "auditory cheesecake" argument

– we would expect it not to last very long in evolutionary time.'

Music has been with us for millennia, Levitin wrote. The earliest human-made artefacts discovered by archaeologists were musical instruments (the oldest found to date, according to my internet trawls, is a 60,000-year-old bone flute found in the Cerkno Hills in Slovenia, made from the femur of a long-extinct European bear). Then we had to consider music's evolutionary role through shared singing, he added. Singing around a campfire helped early man to stay awake and ward off possible predators; it also had behavioural effects, encouraging the development of cooperation and turn-taking practices, strengthening group dynamics.

Levitin then turned his attentions to the brain of the small child. Processing music is 'a form of play', he proposed. 'It encourages different parts of the brain to work together in an integrated way.' It also helps nurture exploratory competence, the natural thrust of curiosity which prepares any child to explore their development of language. The parts of the brain involved in this process include the cerebellum at its base (best known for coordinating movements of the body, and for the connections between motion and emotion) and the cerebral cortex (the outer layer of neural tissue covering the cerebrum, the most evolved part of our brain). The cerebral cortex is the part that processes information, understands language and produces new ideas. It is particularly evolved in humans, distinguishing us from other animals.

Levitin's book jump-started my own explorations further back in time. I discovered the work of Anthony DeCaspar's lab at the University of North Carolina, Greensboro, which he did when I was a small, record-spinning child. Not only did DeCaspar pin down in 1980 the first direct evidence that newborns recognised the maternal voice, but in 1987, he analysed cardiac changes to explain how foetuses experience different basic sounds, like musical tones and syllables. Then I read about Sandra Trehub, director of the pioneering Music Development Lab at the University of Toronto, Mississauga, whose work pinpointed sophisticated listening skills from the early months of life.

Trehub's 2001 paper, 'Musical Predispositions in Infancy', showed how the processing of musical patterns by babies was much like that of adults. '[Babies] do not begin life with a blank musical slate,' she explained. 'Instead, they are predisposed to attend to the melodic contour and rhythmic patterning of sound sequences . . . they are tuned to consonant patterns, melodic as well as harmonic, and to metric rhythms.' Trehub also led a study in 2015 with a group of infants under a year old, where twice the number of the babies were soothed by an adult singing, as opposed to an adult speaking. I thought of me and my grandmother, the radiogram, the warm water, the washing machine.

*

Neuroscientists continue to be fascinated with the links between very young children and music. A leading researcher in the field is Samuel Mehr, director of the Harvard Music Lab, whose work includes studies about diversity in human song, and the way babies respond to lullabies from different musical cultures. I read about how his lab worked with babies one-to-one to track their physical reactions to music, measuring their heart rate and motion, their pupil dilation and gaze.

I email him about my interest in music and babies and we speak on the phone; Mehr is a father of small children himself, and describes how staggering he finds it that the tiniest humans can have such facility with music, far beyond what even the most advanced technology of our times could muster. 'There's a sort of naïve intuition that computers are pretty good at doing simple tasks,' he says. 'Like grabbing some audio and extracting some meaningful information from it, like which part is the melody or which is an instrument playing and which is a voice – but they can't. Those seem like pretty natural tasks for us as humans to do. And even quite little babies are able to solve this really quite complex computational problem.'

We talk about Pinker's idea that music is 'auditory cheesecake', and how that concept is still percolating around academic culture, despite it being rubbished by the likes of Levitin. I try to play devil's advocate with Mehr: doesn't the cheesecake argument explain why all our responses are directed bouncily, instantaneously, towards a song? Mehr responds with a more savoury analogy. 'If we ask ourselves, "Why is it that I enjoy eating a cheese omelette so much?" and we think, "Well, it's nice! It makes me feel good!" – that's still not why we eat it. We eat it because we're hungry. We also eat it because it has protein in it. It tastes good for a number of reasons associated with human evolution, reasons that have nothing to do with making us feel good.' His voice crackles with humour. 'You know, the feeling good is incidental!'

I still love the idea that a song can connect the most advanced parts of our minds with the most mechanical. Somewhere in this series of neural conversations, a song acts as a messenger, uniting our most ancient and most modern selves. A few years after reading Levitin for the first time, I sat with my son, now a toddler, on my lap, in an airy, spaced-out cafe on the high street near our house in East London. 'Super Trouper' came on Radio 2. I sang along to it quietly, but making sure he could hear it, moving his chubby hands high above his head to the melody. When it finished, the DJ said that the working title for the song was '*Blinka Lilla Stjärna*'. In English, this was 'Twinkle Twinkle Little Star'.

I thought of the descending notes of the chorus falling from the sky, and I thought of the emotional lyrics hidden in the naivety of a nursery rhyme. Most of all, I loved that I was still learning from a song I had first heard so many years ago.

*

Before I was a mother, before I realised adulthood had truly settled in, when I was steeling myself to be brave enough to think about having my own family, my mother found a photo of me from November 1980. We knew it was from November 1980, because the date was scribbled on the back in biro. In the photo, I am standing against my grandmother's whitewashed back wall, wearing a bright yellow plastic pinny decorated with blue, red and green fish. My hair is blue-black, my fringe cut by my mother into a blunt donkey-crop. I am wearing a hat of my grandmother's, green and floppy, far too big. My grin is dotted with shiny new teeth. I am two-and-a-half, mischievous, full of delight.

My family look at photos often when we're all together back home. I wonder if it helps us to connect with our old selves, as well as to our changing bonds with each other. As we look at this particular photo, Mam tells me I had stayed with my grandparents for a while around that time. Mam had lost a baby around then, she said, early in pregnancy. She had lost another before me. Dad had been in and out of hospital too, his spondylitis leading to other complications.

Two years after that photo, my baby brother Jon arrived on 5 November. I remember the fireworks at the end of the cul-de-sac where we lived, and I think of some of the other music I loved early on in my life, like the pop songs of Culture Club, and the Kids from Fame soundtrack. The memories of this music sit like pretty clouds around my head, animations from a misty-eyed Disney film, surrounding me like my own weather system.

I wonder if I have always found music to be a provider of warmth, and a warmth that I can hold onto in tough times. Perhaps I connect it in my memory to the warmth in that sink water, and the significance of my hands in that water, as I tried to spin my own sounds. Music gave me a place to put my feelings and control them, especially when I felt lonely or when everything around me felt too much. Music helped me not to feel blue.

*

In my late thirties, 'Super Trouper' would come to mean something different again to me. Stuck in a rainy train station one late summer's afternoon in 2017, I got a phone call from an exhibition organiser at London's Southbank Centre. They were going to be staging an ABBA exhibition, starting in December. It was going to be called *Super Troupers*. They needed a scriptwriter. The script would be read by a celebrity reader. The script reader was Jarvis Cocker. The scriptwriter, if I'd agree to the fee, would be me.

The train to Cardiff Central pulled into the platform opposite. Instantly, I was on a coach to Cardiff Central twenty-two autumns earlier, with four friends, refreshed by a cheap bottle of peach-flavoured wine that we'd passed around. Then I was on the short walk to the university students' union to see Jarvis Cocker with Pulp, a band once described on an early press release as a cross between ABBA and The Fall. That night – 15 October 1995 – they sang to our futures, to discos in the year 2000, to people with whom you wanted to have babies.

That night, my friend Claire and I threw a pair of huge knickers at Jarvis, bought from a stall in my local market, decorated with our biro-scribbled landline phone numbers. Jarvis had caught the knickers and hung them on his microphone stand for the remainder of the gig. We wondered nervously all the way home what would happen if he phoned and our mothers answered.

'Would you like to do it? We need an answer quite quickly.' Rainy station. 2017. I screamed yes.

*

For the next two months, I spent my life steeped in ABBA. I delved into the merry-go-rounds of *Ring Ring*, the wayward glitz of *Waterloo*. I took in the tremulous shimmer of *Arrival*, the precise disco sheen of *Voulez-Vous* and the opaque intensity of *The Visitors*. My job was to lead ABBA's fans through seven rooms in the exhibition that told the story of their career. Jarvis would be reading the words I had given him, and the exhibition would start with a bulky, knackered-looking piece of equipment: a Super Trouper spotlight itself.

With Jarvis's voice in my head as I wrote, I travelled through the folk festival scene from which they had emerged; the murkiness of three-day-week Britain into which they arrived like shiny cavaliers; the band's imperial disco moments and their rare international tours; their summer retreats in leafy archipelagos with their sons and daughters; to the end of the decade when everything unravelled. Two weeks before the exhibition opened, the script recording with Jarvis went well. I didn't tell him about my knickers.

A few days later, news came in from Sweden. Björn Ulvaeus himself was coming over for the mid-December press launch, which was unexpected. Members of ABBA didn't often make public appearances. This meant I would be able to shake the hand of the person who set my first memory in motion, the hand that first worked out the notes of 'Super Trouper' on a guitar while Benny played along on the piano, notes that rose out of Grandpa's radiogram one autumn day in 1980.

But the day before my morning train to London, snow fell heavily at my home, now in Wales. Our road became a snake of black ice. The temperature hit minus eleven. At six a.m., when I was meant to leave, the snow was still falling. London had missed the deluge, meaning the show would go on.

Suddenly I became a child again, trying to paint a new picture. Perhaps the thick, snowy torrents could turn into softer bubbles of launderette soap. Perhaps the sky could suddenly transform from darkness into oceans of Amami blue. Then a whirr could enter my ears, not from the sound of a twin tub washing machine, but the helicopter on the cover of ABBA's *Arrival*. Björn could land in my garden, open the door to my air taxi and stretch out his hand.

Later that morning, I was standing in my kitchen, drinking coffee, watching as the hands of the clock passed the time of the launch. The old stool I used to stand on was still out from the morning, when my son, now three-and-a-half, had washed his hands. He was outside with his daddy just beyond the open back door, not far from our shed, making snowmen and smiling. The radio was playing in the kitchen, as it always does, a habit I had picked up and retained from my grandparents.

I thought of all the songs that had come from it already this morning, wondering if any had grabbed my little boy and cemented a proper memory. I turned on the tap and filled up the tub for my mug. The day suddenly shone like the sun.

Track 2
Only You – The Flying Pickets

How Music Kick-Starts Distant Memories

Before I move on to the time in my life when my father was a recollection I had to fight for, an image constantly losing definition, I have to return to the last song that was truly ours. This song does something to me when it suddenly appears, as if it's arriving out of nowhere and everywhere – from a radio, a TV advert, a car window, a shop's sound system. For years I've wanted to understand the emotional power it unleashes within me.

It isn't 'Pipes of Peace' by Paul McCartney. It's the song that was at number one just before, another giddy horse in the race around my father's last request.

This song leapt out at me with a particular violence a few years ago, in the cold and dark early weeks of December. I was deep in Abergavenny, our nearest town, swaddled like a baby in my thick winter coat, burrowing through bodies filling busy pavements and shop-aisles, bags carving indentations into my fingers. My last-minute stocking filler list for my family was no longer clear to me, striking a regular pattern in my head; it was now phasing, shifting, distorting.

I tunnelled through the heaviness of the season, longing for the shop doors to open, and to breathe, and I breathed. I always find comfort when I've got out, when I can feel air and not people around me; then I feel totally myself, even if it's only for a moment, alone.

And that's when I heard it.

Ba-da-da-da.

Ba-da-da-da.

It had arrived uninvited, with the full force of a tornado.

Suddenly I was wrenched away from the gloomy evening, whipped into another dimension, before being dropped into a very different place – but one that felt strangely familiar. I was suddenly in colour, in a landscape of faded browns, oranges and greys, opening a front door to . . . a cold Monday morning. Sleepy-wide, dark brown eyes. Shiny-blue-black hair. A familiar smile.

He is only ever there for a short time when he returns. If I'm lucky, we talk about school, and the book that I am reading with Mrs Howells in Year 1; it is green, Level 9 Book 3 on the Ginn Reading Scheme, with a witch swimming in the sea on its cover. It is the book my headmaster talked to me about as I walked up the school hall to my grandma in his office, to take me home, on the day that Dad died, to my mother sitting behind the net curtains in the front room. I found an old copy years later on eBay, and bought it, reading its pages like runes, trying and failing to find some divine messages.

Sometimes we talk about Jon, my little brother, who I love, who has just started to crawl, but more often than not, I just tell him that the song that was number one over Christmas isn't number one any more. I'd learn later that it was a cover of a song originally written and performed by the pop duo Yazoo, and not by those Welshmen at all.

Ba-da-da-da.

Ba-da-da-da.

And just like that, as an adult thought intrudes and breaks the spell, he's gone again. I'm in the street, the wind cold, 'Only You' playing itself out. My skin feels alert; my pulse is racing. To everyone else, I'm a woman in a shop doorway, overtaken by the stress of Christmas shopping. Inside, I am separating from my five-year-old self, trying not to shrink back into her completely.

*

'Only You' by Yazoo was released in 1982. Yazoo comprised Vince Clarke, who wrote it, and Alison Moyet, who sang it, her voice as deep and resilient as the sea. In its original, 'Only You' sounds like a song about a relationship that has ended, where someone's needs weren't being met. Its lyrics reflect on contact and closeness and the loss of both of these things, and a protagonist not able to cope with these brutal realities.

Moyet's vocals soak the song's sentiments in sadness but also a mood of solemn resignation. 'It's getting harder to stay,' she sings, 'when I see you.' All she needed was the love he gave; it was all she needed for another day.

The version of 'Only You' that my dad liked, however, wasn't by Alison and Vince. It was the festive a cappella version by The Flying Pickets, released a year later. It's a desperately uncool cover, and I love its implication that my dad wasn't particularly interested in fashion. I'm a similar soul, as excited by the songs referred to as bubblegum and cheese as those considered more delicate, tasteful and refined. The Flying Pickets' version of 'Only You' also affects me more than Yazoo's because of who the Flying Pickets were: a collection of jobbing, singing actors from South Wales.

For many Welsh people, the sound of ordinary men singing together prompts a visceral response, thanks to our tradition of choirs. Around 1984, Welsh men were not known for expressing deep emotions one-to-one. They didn't do this at work or at home or over pints in the workingmen's club, but when you stood near them on a Sunday as an organ struck up the opening bars of a hymn, or saw them standing together on a stage in a welfare hall, shoulder-to-shoulder, about to sing the *Elijah* or *Messiah*, you knew what was going to happen. Their chests would expand in one collective breath, songs acting on them all as defibrillators.

The Flying Pickets weren't as commanding as a male voice choir, of course, but the way they looked was consoling to me: they were unglamorous, dark-haired, short and squat. They were also making music in the middle of the miners' strike. Songs were often sung as men emerged from the mineshafts, leaving behind all that danger, darkness and dirt.

But, of course, I mainly loved the Flying Pickets' 'Only You' because my dad loved the Flying Pickets' 'Only You'. For a long time, I had to run away from it every Christmas: its immediate cut then its lingering bruise was too much. The song seemed to disappear in the 2000s – not having as much star-spangled wattage as nineties confections by Mariah and East 17 to stand out for the radio schedules – but then came streaming services, playlist culture and festive radio stations embracing 24-7 seasonality. 'Only You' now seems to arrive often, in flurries, every winter.

I wonder what Dad would have made of the rest of the Top 10 that week: of Howard Jones, Kenny Rogers and Dolly Parton, Status Quo, the Thompson Twins. When I was young, I used to think of the charts as a reflection of the messy world that we lived in, full of disparate genres all mixed up together. All human life was there among the Top 40 climbers, the newcomers, the fallers, the stayers. Very famous people, like former Beatles, would reach the summit or get close to it quite often, but occasionally a group of deeply ordinary characters did too.

Perhaps one ordinary man hoped that ordinary moment might have lasted a little longer.

Ba-da-da-da.
Ba-da-da-da.

*

Songs excite and exercise our brains in our earliest years, but they also take us *back* to our earliest years, and do it quickly. In 2009, Professor Petr Janata of the University of California, Davis, discovered something new and surprising about the brain that might explain why. He'd recently discovered that the medial prefrontal cortex – part of the more evolved front portion of the brain – was responsible for tracking the movement of melodies in songs. Previously, this had been thought to be the job of the auditory cortex, which dealt in a very straightforward manner with the way we receive and process sound. (Or as Pinker might put it with regards to music, like a greedy mouse after pudding.)

Other research was being done on the medial prefrontal cortex, outside music tracking and processing, in 2009. Janata was interested in studies that suggested that this part of the brain was also integral to the preservation of a person's sense of self and how they view and define themselves. He had a hunch. Given that the processing of our identities and the processing of music happened in the same part of the brain, perhaps this could explain how musical memories carried such profound baggage.

Janata set up a study, playing thirteen of his university students thirty-second clips of songs while under an fMRI scanner. He had chosen these from the *Billboard* Top 100 from a time when his subjects were between eight and eighteen years of age, far away enough in time to trigger a memory. He set up a school disco of the mind, not under a glitterball but the gleam of a brain-mapping machine. If any sample triggered an autobiographical memory, the students had to describe to the researchers what that memory was.

Janata's hunch proved correct: the songs that promoted the most neural activity in the medial prefrontal cortex were those that prompted vivid recollections. 'A piece of familiar music [therefore] serves as a soundtrack for a mental movie that starts playing in our head,' Janata confirmed to *Live Science* later that year. 'It calls back memories of a particular person or place, and you might all of a sudden see that person's face in your mind's eye.'

After reading about Janata's work, I find one of his lectures on YouTube. Here is a serious soul, but his suit and tie look nicely eccentric. His mop of white and black curls suggests a member of Sparks or The Cars rather than a conventional academic. I find his email on his university website, and send him a message on a darkening late autumn afternoon when I am away from home, desperately trying to write. Only an hour after I press send, a reply pings into my inbox. That same November evening, we speak on the phone about music, him in his sunny West Coast office, me at a twilit desk in rainy Shropshire.

Janata is happy to walk me slowly through his work, in solid academic sentences. He is kind with his time. His interest in music came not just from his interest in neuroscience, he explains, which was what I'd suspected. He'd been surrounded by music as a child, mainly classical at first, as his parents both played the piano. He'd then learned the instrument himself, and enjoyed music theory especially, because it taught him how music was formally organised.

As an adolescent, he got into rock and pop. 'It wasn't until then that I actually realised that there was such a thing as Top 40 radio,' he laughs. The Beatles, Simon & Garfunkel and Grateful Dead were Janata's teenage bands, and they were still his adult bands too: he plays piano and keyboards in groups, where he enjoys playing their songs. 'I'm not a songwriter myself,' he says, half-apologetically. 'There are a lot of covers going on. But it feels special, playing music with other people. And going out to band practice on a weekly basis . . . I call that my field research.'

Janata already had songs in his own life that evoked deep memories before he set up his studies. His parents were Czech immigrants to the US, and Czech folk songs still catapult him to road trips back in the country where his parents grew up. Simon & Garfunkel's 'The Sound of Silence' takes him to his college days in Austria when he was an exchange student trying to learn the song on the guitar ('and failing miserably at my attempts to do so'). 'Mrs. Robinson' reminds him of the time he saw *The Graduate* back in the States, as well as the cinema in which he saw it, and of his friends from that period in the late sixties.

He speculates that music most commonly takes people back to general periods of their life, rather than notable events. 'Often a song has been a soundtrack for them during a particular summer or even during a particular year at school, or a period hanging out with a specific group of friends, or a time spent with significant others. This is why the teenage years, for many people, are quite common triggers for these memories.'

But my memory of 'Only You' and my father is more specific, and connected to a much earlier time in my life; I pluck up the courage to mention it. Janata says he is very sorry for my loss, then explains how painful memories can also act as sponges for songs.

One person in his study struck him specifically, he says. A young woman who had recognised several pieces of music: 'She saw these songs trace the trajectory of the relationship with her first boyfriend. With one, she initially remembered being very much in love. With another, he was a year older, off to college, and she was still in high school: she remembered talking on the phone to him a lot. Then this song came up that took her back to when she discovered that he was cheating on her.' She described the song in detail in her notes. 'She said I reminded her of her epiphany that all men are lying, cheating dogs and bastards!'

What moved Janata most about the study, he says, was the potency of memories when familiar music was being played – how the fMRI scanner came to life – and how consistently this seemed to happen in very different people. 'We form very strong memories for the music itself. Think about when you're singing to yourself and not producing any sound too – it's all just inside your head. We can establish these music memory traces so strongly. There are so many associations formed with the contents of other memories, and music serves as a really effective retrieval cue.'

He mentions another song that always takes him back to a conference dinner in Budapest, where he was doing a project that was very important to him: a version of Antônio Carlos Jobim's 'The Girl from Ipanema'. 'I just vividly remember that restaurant setting, the arrangement of the song. Every detail.' One person's conference dinner restaurant is another person's front door.

When we end the call, I type 'Only You' into the search bar on my Spotify account, add 'Flying Pickets', slide the volume right up into my headphones, click play. It isn't yet December, so it feels wrong from the start, but playing it affords a very different feeling. I have sought it out, hunted it down, skewered it: I am a hunter making sure its prey has completely succumbed. Some of the lyrics and harmonies still prompt twinges of sadness, but they are much easier to control. Perhaps I am in charge of the memory now. Maybe I am the song's master.

*

A month after I speak to Janata, a few days before Christmas, I am watching BBC4 while trying to wrap a mountain of presents. I'm a Grinch throughout Advent, winter being my least favourite season, so I have to try and engineer festive spirit; sometimes only archive clip shows will do. 'Only You' suddenly comes on. Its arrival is unexpected. The opening notes feel icy and sharp. Then I see the singers. They are dressed as fat-bellied snowmen, with the surreal addition of weapons-grade New Romantic make-up. Frontman Brian Hibbard's eyes are smudged with eyeliner; he looks like a saggy Marc Almond with a mullet plopped on top, spray-on snow on his fringe and a red bauble as an earring completing the ensemble. A hat-wearing snowman behind him has cheeks like strawberry circles, rouged on top of white panstick, his mouth lined in gothic black lipstick. He is also gripping a pipe in his teeth as he tries to *ba-da-da-da, ba-da-da-da*.

Watching that performance feels like a hilarious, surreal exorcism. When I hear the song next, I think, perhaps this is what I'll see. An old, sad memory will be spat out of my VHS-vintage brain and be replaced by a vision of a gaggle of men in a TV studio in bad fancy dress.

It is strange to think that a memory might be so easily changed by something so ridiculous – and time would prove that my memory would never metamorphose entirely. But as I got older, I was realising that memories are not dusty video-cassettes in a cupboard, waiting to be converted and cleaned. They are constantly reconstructed every time we recall them, as a 2016 *Atlantic* report by Pulitzer Prize-winning science journalist Ed Yong underlined in blunt detail.

In his piece, 'Memory Lane Has a Three-Way Fork', Yong explains the parts of the brain that have to work together to recreate our memories. First comes the hippocampus, the tiny, seahorse-shaped part of the brain near the top of the brain stem. A case study in 1953 showed how vital the hippocampus was: neuroscientist William Beecher Scoville removed it from an epileptic patient, Henry Molaison, who then lost many of his old memories, and was unable to create new ones. This is how it would be for all of us, Yong explained, and why the hippocampus is known colloquially as the 'seat of memory'.

Yong then detailed a study by Cambridge University professor Jon Simons, which explained more about what happens after the hippocampus is stirred into action. In this study, the subjects were shown distinctive images, then asked to recall them again later, under an fMRI scanner, in as much detail as possible.

When the subjects recalled any image at all, the hippocampus lit up. If they recalled something with precision, an area located higher up in the brain, called the angular gyrus, became active. If the memories were particularly vivid, the precuneus, further back and towards the surface of the brain, went into overdrive. 'Very roughly speaking, the hippocampus kicks the process off, the angular gyrus does the heavy lifting, and the precuneus gives us that vibrant, first-person sense of actually remembering something,' Yong wrote.

Memory isn't just an act of retrieval, but a process of constant reconnection and reconstruction, Yong continued. Memory is therefore liable to be reshaped and reformed, even if we try to resist reshaping and reforming it. There is a cruel irony in this activity, of course. While we fight for memory to be unyielding and true, we are constantly reframing it in the contexts in which we are living at that moment – a revelation I found deeply unsettling.

I wanted the memory of my father to be solid. But beyond my immediate reaction to 'Only You', I had always worried about how much of what I remembered at the front door was real. Reading Yong made this uneasiness even more pronounced. I'd been able to pin down my misty memories of 'Super Trouper' thanks to my grandma, but there was no witness to my last moment with my dad. I'd kept telling myself that this memory had become locked away, far from the detritus we accumulate as we get older. My experience in a shop doorway while Christmas shopping also confirmed for me that memory is never simply locked away. It can be opened any time, any place, presumably for anyone.

*

Not long after, I stumble across the work of Professor Catherine Loveday on Twitter. She's a neuropsychologist at the University of Westminster who does fascinating work on reminiscence bumps: the periods of our lives in which we recall songs most vividly. I message her, and she sends me some links to her work, including a TEDx talk. Within minutes of watching it, I know I have to speak to her.

Loveday begins the talk with an anecdote about going Christmas shopping, having a lovely time with her husband, then suddenly hearing the Johnny Mathis song 'When a Child Is Born' playing somewhere. She finds herself 'overwhelmed with emotion, tears rolling down her cheeks . . . a complete mess'. The song takes her back to her childhood Christmases, she wrote, describing the feeling as being overwhelmed with 'grief, nostalgia and happiness . . . a strange mix'. It was her late stepfather's favourite song, one that fostered within her family a real sense of belonging.

We Zoom. I tell her about me and 'Only You'. She smiles. 'You get this completely visceral response, don't you? It can be a song you know well, but usually, it's a song you haven't listened to for ages, and you have this brief moment where you are absolutely back in time, and it's so fleeting that you can't grab it, and you're back again, and you can never quite get it back.'

I talk about our responses to these songs being involuntary. How does that happen? 'I think we are reactivating synaptic connections,' she begins, before going back to basics to describe to me how memory works. 'Essentially, when you experience anything, like smelling a rose, a very unique set of neurons will fire in a very unique pattern. Absolutely every sensory experience we have fires a unique set. And when those things fire together a few times, they become functionally linked, so you have a pattern that is always recognised. What I think is happening with music is that you are getting that pattern recognition – you haven't actively sought to remember something, but you have reactivated enough cells in that network that the whole thing has come alive.'

Included in the network of that initial memory, she adds, is everything else that was happening at that time, because an experience is multi-sensory: a set of sights and smells and sounds. 'So in effect, for me, that song plays, one thing fires, and it's linked to the cells that represent my stepdad – it triggers those connections. Memories are essentially networks of functionally linked cells, and even though you can choose to activate them – by actively thinking, "Oh, what did we used to do at Christmas time?" or "What did Dad enjoy listening to?" – something can come in from nowhere and just trigger that memory for you.'

Loveday has the same reaction to Johnny Mathis every year without willing it on. 'Every year, the first time that song appears, that intense emotional reaction happens again.' But something else is also fired in the brain when we hear these songs, she says, something people don't often appreciate: our brain's capacity to project ideas of ourselves into the future.

'When we inhabit the past, we really take it on, whether we want to or not. But in our heads, we have also existed in the future with that person.' Loveday has a visual analogy that helps her think about this idea. In it, she is herself, a person standing on the top of a big hill, like Primrose Hill in London, with a cityscape surrounding her. The cityscape is her life, full of details, reaching far into the distance. Some features overpower the landscape, like the BT Tower or the Shard – we have people who perform similar functions to these buildings, she says – they grab attention more than others who blend into the background. Events can work in the same way.

It doesn't matter where Loveday stands in that landscape. Those huge landmarks will always have a presence, and even if they suddenly disappear one day – knocked down overnight – she will still remember the might of them when they've gone. 'You don't realise how much time you've spent in that landscape until it changes.' I imagine myself searching for the BT Tower from Primrose Hill and not finding it, thinking how discombobulating that could be. I think of myself as a little girl peering out of our front door, imagining the man who had stood there returning to me.

Loveday also thinks music can play a big role in our unconscious memories. I talk about how old I was when my dad died. She brings up her other dad – her real dad, she says – who died when she was six (her mother later remarried). When she used to think about him, Mike Oldfield's 'Tubular Bells' often played in her mind, a piece of music that made her feel emotional, even though she couldn't link it to a specific memory. Early memories are often fragmentary, she adds; a child's conscious memory doesn't really kick in consistently until they are five or six, anyway, 'the point at which you and I lost our fathers'.

We retain unconscious memories from before that age, however. 'I mean, I don't consciously remember my father liking 'Tubular Bells', but, when I mentioned to an old friend, who knew him very well, that the song made me think about him, she said, "Oh, he loved that, he bought the album, he played it all the time." So, somewhere in my unconscious, I had made that association, without any direct knowledge that he liked it.'

This unconscious memory system also remains 'totally robust right the way through our lifetime,' Loveday says. It stretches well into old age, and many people with dementia still have it functioning well. There are many other unconscious memories that don't stop us in our tracks or make us think about the past: walking is an unconscious memory, for example. We don't have to think about how to do it, nor remember how we learned it. 'This means your body can remember something that your conscious mind cannot access. You learn to make this connection between things without having any conscious knowledge of the learning experience.'

When Loveday hears her father's or her stepfather's songs, she confesses that she often indulges herself in the emotions she is going through. 'You can move away from this kind of memory, but there's also something beautifully nostalgic and alluring about it that draws me in and makes me want to stop what I'm doing and embrace everything that goes with it.'

I am honest with myself for a moment. Yes, I felt a deep sadness when I was Christmas shopping that night – a peculiar, deep ache – but I also let myself fall into the feelings, so I could feel that crackle of familiar electrical impulses, experience that recognisable release.

'Music wraps you up and comforts you and holds you in a way that not many things do. It's really weird, isn't it? So fascinating. I feel like I'm being held by this piece of music. Do you?'

I tell Loveday I do.

*

My mother's WhatsApp message arrives one night just before tea. She has been up in the attic and has found something.

She has taken a few photographs of a piece of cardboard. It is white and shiny on one side, buff and tough on the other. It probably began life slid inside a packet of sheer tights, bought at the chemist on the high street, or a pair of thick socks, rolled up to ward off the winter.

Mam has laid the cardboard on the sofa, lifted her smartphone, snapped a few photos and sent them. I wonder if she has thought about the consequences of those small movements of her fingers. She has captured a folkloric object in megapixels. She's stopped a fragmented memory feeling like a hallucination.

This piece of cardboard was folded in half, by me, when I was five years old – five years, eight months and twelve days old, to be precise. After I folded the cardboard in half, I then took a biro to it and started drawing on it.

I look at the makeshift greetings card now on the small screen. In the front of one photo is a picture of Father Christmas with dashes for eyes, and a Christmas tree. Its branches are thin, pointy spikes. Father Christmas has a speech bubble sticking out of the left of his mouth, like a helium balloon or a stop sign. 'Sssh!' the word inside it says.

In another photo, inside the card, there are two drawings. One is of a man in a bed, alone. The bed's legs stick out metallically, like robot limbs. An upside-down V is his moustache. A huge U is his smile. The man has sticks for arms, stretched out at right angles to his body, drawn like children often draw people, as if they're extended for a hug. The ink around the character is smudged by small, chubby hands. The other picture is of a wonky oblong with another wonky oblong inside: a television. I had written five words inside it. The Flying Pickets. Only You.

Get Well Soon Daddy, say the other words around it. See You Soon Daddy. I Love You. Thirty Xs, drawn carefully, sit next to a man about to be anaesthetised in a hospital room.

This is a card I must have written to my father the evening after I had seen him for the last time before he would unexpectedly die. It is a card that sends a message to me, and by extension to him: that I hadn't forgotten about what he'd asked me to do. It is an extra message, an extra story.

It is a card I don't remember, but a card that pins together old, misty recollections in hard copy, in a way that my mind never could. I wrote it on the Monday night, my mother confirms, and she took it into the hospital on the Tuesday. Dad read it on his last full day in the world.

This card hasn't been constantly reconstructed over the years, or constantly remade by neural conversations. It has been sitting in a box, surrounded by three decades of dust, waiting for someone to pop the lid open.

Dad had loved pop music. I had loved pop music. I had always told myself that the connection between us was strong. I can't tell you how much it meant to me that at the heart of my last message to him, beating strong, was a song.

Track 3

Prince Charming – Adam and the Ants

How Music Opens Up Our Childhoods

After Dad died, I used to tell myself the music stopped. There is a misty shape of a holiday seven months later, in August 1984, to Saundersfoot, West Wales, where my mother, baby brother and I had gone the previous summer with my father. On that holiday, I'd fallen down the steps of our hotel on the beach, smashed my teeth on the pebbles, running to Dad for comfort. Any thought of the next holiday makes my memories glitch. My grandparents came with us, and I think of them as strange apparitions in the sea. Long stretches of jellyfish glow on the shoreline, and my baby brother, by then nearly two, toddles around them and the wet edges of the water. I am often in the middle of the scene, my mouth still sore, streaked with blood.

When I think of the mid-eighties, I think of disasters on news bulletins and in Grandpa's *Daily Mirror*, the *People* and *News of the World*. I remember a May afternoon watching *Grandstand* with him, pink wafers on a plate on the armchair by the TV, an orange haze under the benches of a football stadium, the sudden biblical sea of flames at Bradford City, the old man emerging from the stands, on fire, the TV cameras zooming in. Later, the old man died. I remember thinking that maybe that was my dad, appearing divinely like a god, before disappearing again.

When I think of those years, I remember the shuttle going into space with the school teacher on board who had the same perm as my mother, then watching the shuttle exploding on *Newsround*. I think of the weather forecast just before my eighth birthday, and the worries about acid rain floating across from Chernobyl to the sheep farms of mid-Wales, the atomic threat, the prospect of nuclear war. I think of other names that became metonyms for human horror – Zeebrugge, Enniskillen, Clapham Junction, Lockerbie, Kegworth, Hillsborough – and how I became obsessed with the places behind them, where people had experienced unthinkable things.

I didn't realise I needed help from other people either until help came along. Or, should I say, until *they* came along: the people from different, fantastical realms that opened up my childhood.

Outside my family, the person I loved most when I was seven was standing on a balcony when I saw him for the first time. His chin was up, two slashes of red painting his sculpted right cheek. He was dressed like a prince, but not the one who had married Princess Diana, for whom we had a party on the roundabout at the end of our road when I was three, full of fondant fancies and egg-and-cress sandwiches speared with little blue and red flags, as old photographs tell me. This prince wore a black jacket with gold buttons and had black hair in tight plaits and he was swinging on a chandelier towards me, towards me.

The presenter said he was Adam Ant, from London. I was Judith Rogers, from Swansea. I wanted to stand like him, leap like him – become him.

*

Pop songs brought glamorous, alternative father figures into my life when I needed them most. They carried them into my consciousness without invitation. I let them in happily, invested myself in them, especially the ones that felt exuberant and extravagant.

The first boys I loved came before Adam, but not by long. I have to give them a proper part in my story because they are the first thing I remember, with any solidity, after the loss of my father.

They arrived in my ears in the girls' changing rooms at school, when I was trying to tie my shoelaces, making a loop then another, my little clumsy hands trying to get them to work together. A radio had been left on in the corridor by the gym cleaners, from which a tune suddenly flew out. This is the first time I can recall the intense physical process of listening to and instantly loving a song.

When we hear something, anything, sound waves sneak into our ears, vibrating three tiny bones, our hammer, anvil and stirrup. These then vibrate the eardrum and the tiny hairs in our cochlea, a spiral tube in our inner ear which looks like a shell of a snail. Electrical signals are sent from here to our nervous system, which start neural conversations between the animalistic and more evolved parts of our brains. Together, they try to process these tiny aural messages, the pitch, rhythm and tone of these sounds, to anticipate what is coming next, and this still happens today when I listen to Wham!'s October 1984 single, 'Freedom', the song I heard as I struggled with my shoelaces at school.

It's a song I still play all the time to turbo-power happy feelings. I love how its opening three-note riff demands a dramatic act of finger-pointing. I love how it canters on top of a lithe, light bassline. I love George Michael's over-enthusiastic delivery and its Chic-like guitars. I don't care that the song got mixed reviews at the time. David

Quantick – whose writing I'd later love as a teenager – called it 'annoying . . . fake Motown . . . wildly empty'. For me, it is a loving, tender homage, packed with riffs, wildly full. It also has one of the greatest bridges ever from the verse to the chorus, a bridge that begs, pleads and yearns, motoring along on a fast and hard beat that I air-drum along to every time without fail or embarrassment. It was written by a man who had written some of his biggest hits on the dole, in his bedroom and on buses around Watford. This adds to my love of his music every time I hear it, once, twice, for ever.

Soon after, I found out who Wham! were on Saturday morning TV, the same way I'd later learn about my facepainted and plait-wearing prince. I loved George and his school-friend Andrew Ridgeley: they looked like two lifelong buddies having the time of their lives. Their firm bond took me far away from my existence as a little girl and a loner, trying to fit in in the schoolyard, knowing I wasn't like everyone else. I remember seeing the 'Wake Me Up Before You Go-Go' video around the same time and how it suddenly made everything feel all right. How could it not? George was a golden-haired smile bouncing down a catwalk in a T-shirt that screamed two words in capital letters: CHOOSE LIFE.

Choose Life. How could you choose it? Didn't we already have it? Maybe not. This life was something else, surely. Something new.

George and Andrew looked self-possessed, confident and convincing together. Their hairdos seemed to be guest-starring on episodes of *Dynasty* and *Dallas* simultaneously. I loved their naughty boy routine on the video to

'Club Tropicana', playing silver trumpets in tiny trunks, falling off lilos, tipping drinks into ripples of bright, swishy swimming pool. Nowadays, that video looks like an advert for conspicuous consumption rather than the fluffy parody which was intended. But none of this mattered to me back then, naturally. I saw two friends wearing cowboy hats, riding donkeys. I saw accessible film stars.

Of course, this concept was precisely engineered. In *I'm Coming To Take You Out To Lunch*, his book about his time as manager of Wham!, Simon Napier-Bell describes spotting the duo on *Top of the Pops* after they made their first album. 'They'd sung and danced with an extraordinary macho exuberance,' he wrote, 'yet there seemed to be a strange intimacy flowing between them . . . and they had a wonderful image – pure Hollywood – *Butch Cassidy and the Sundance Kid* or *Starsky & Hutch*.' Napier-Bell famously took Wham! to China in April 1985, making them the first Western duo to perform in the Communist country. He realised that their brand of freedom could be translated and sold.

The video to the US release of 'Freedom', in mid-1985, is made up of footage that would eventually become part of a film about that trip, *Wham! In China: Foreign Skies*. I watched the full documentary on YouTube recently, cross-legged on my bed. Amazingly, it was directed by Lindsay Anderson, maker of *If . . .* and *O Lucky Man*. (He said in an interview at the time that he only did it for the money.)

It's gauche and cheesy, of course, but also fascinating to watch. Among the temples and the market stalls and the fleets of bicycles crossing a square that would turn out to be Tiananmen, we see people from different countries and political regimes observing each other tentatively, edgily. The newly arrived grinning boys make the Chinese ministers visibly nervous. At one point, George Michael, still only twenty-one, sweet and thoughtful throughout, says something brilliant about the unsettling energy of pop, something that reminds you why this music is always banned in repressive regimes. 'A lot of people, the younger people, are very excited about the gig. And obviously, there are those that are older that think it is the beginning of the end.'

*

Wham! became my heroes, initially, because of the sound of their songs (Adam and the Ants' music would impact more fiercely, rowdily, noisily upon me a little later). Their tunes were a great entry-point for pop, a series of brightly coloured singalong creations, offering new landscapes for my escapist infant imagination to fill.

Still, I've always wondered why certain musical elements of 'Freedom', as the first song I loved, grabbed me that afternoon. A snatch of notes here, a chord change there, had effected a huge transformation. I turned to a 2011 book, *The Music Instinct*, by science writer Philip Ball, to try to figure out why.

Philip Ball's range of knowledge about the world is vast. He has written books about colour in art, medieval architecture, the history of invisibility, water in China and physics in Nazi Germany. I first spoke to him for a piece about patterns in nature I was writing for a magazine in 2017, about the rules that govern termite mounds, hives and honeycombs. He knew a lot about that, too. He was also fascinated by patterns in music, I discovered, and how to unpick them.

The Music Instinct explores many facets of the organisation of sound, including how melodies follow rules that we learn to respond to. It tells us how songwriters often use tricks that try to transport our attention, like the semitone rise in key towards the end of Stevie Wonder's 'You Are the Sunshine of My Life', or the whole-tone rise when the last chorus is repeated in the Beatles' 'Penny Lane'. 'Typically these shifts come shortly before the end of a song, just when momentum is starting to flag,' Ball explains, before raising an eyebrow. 'It can be used to the point of cliché, becoming a way of the songwriter to snatch unearned impetus.' I liked his sly, cheeky style.

A key change is something most of us are able to spot by the age of seven, Ball adds. Even before that, at five or six, most children can sing a song vaguely in a key, without musical training. They can also understand musical tonality at this age, Ball continues, like the structure of a seven-note major scale; this sounds improbable, before you consider once again our exposure to sounds in the womb.

Whatever system of tonality we understand depends on our social and cultural surroundings, however. In other words, children like the child that I was will respond more to the seven-note major scale because it is the language of the classical music and pop music that surrounded me at home. Children in non-Western countries may respond to other scale systems, depending on the musical cultures that have bubbled up around them.

At six, I loved 'Freedom' because of its music alone, its effervescent major-key buoyancy. I didn't know that the lyric was about a man wanting his girlfriend to be with him and no one else – and that lyric still doesn't matter to me now. I love 'Freedom' because of its melody and its big leaps in intervals – the spaces between the pitches of its notes – and how it feels like its tune is always vaulting thrillingly high in the air, rarely getting ready to land.

As someone who learned piano and violin as a child, I'll try not to disappear in music theory, but describe the movements of this melody very simply. In the first line of the chorus, when George sings 'I don't want your' and then 'freedom', he moves from the base note of the scale to a minor seventh: a leap of almost an octave. An octave is the distance between one note – say a middle C on the piano – and the C above it. To not quite get there is to be incredibly close to resolution.

George repeats the phrase in the penultimate line of the chorus, but the interval now stretches to a ninth, just *above* the resolving octave. It feels like a perilous, but more hopeful place to be – I still feel left hanging every time I hear it, waiting for the melody to fall – and then it does, and all is well with the world. But there is something else going on when songwriters play with these ideas. The establishment of a pattern of leaps means a song has created its own world, with its own internal logic, Ball writes. Leaps also keep us interested.

If we were to use only small pitch steps [in songwriting], then music would be rather dull . . . [but] these big jumps have to be kept under control, as it were, so that the song doesn't sound like wild yodelling. One of the ways that is done is by following them soon after with other large jumps . . . [and] composers and songwriters have come to recognise that large changes in pitch shouldn't be placed in isolation among little steps. The repetition is, in effect, a way for the composer to 'rewrite the rules'.

'Freedom''s command of my ear never lessens in its energy because I love anticipating what's coming next within its familiar structure. I discover online that theories of musical anticipation and expectation have excited neuroscientists for decades. A foundational text is Leonard Meyer's 1956 book *Emotion and Meaning in Music*, in which Meyer explores how our brains gain satisfaction while predicting a song's repetitions and deviations. A more recent paper, David Huron's 'Sweet Anticipation: music and the psychology of expectation' from 2007, takes this idea much further, suggesting five response systems in our brains that fire up when music starts to play.

Firstly, there is the reaction/defensive response system, which occurs when we first hear a song. Then comes a tension response system, when the brain is trying to discern what is going on, detecting disturbances in the regular flow of rhythm, or unusual cadences at the ends of musical phrases. Then come the more positive systems of prediction (wondering where a piece of music could go), imagination (opening up to ourselves the myriad possibilities of this process), then appraisal (how happy we are that we've correctly identified some patterns).

When our brain processes melodies, it is 'search[ing] for coherence in the stimuli it perceives', Ball writes in his book. I wonder if 'Freedom' spoke to me because it presented a sequence of huge, choreographed jumps, the aural equivalent of a gymnastics display, before it landed on its feet and achieved, for me at least, a perfect ten. It was mimicking the huge lurches within my internal life, showing that I could survive all of them gracefully, smile at the judges, raise my hands in the air.

*

I find Philip's email in my inbox from that previous journalism assignment, and decide to tell him how much I liked his book. It made me think about a pop song that I loved when I was young, I type, and how its melody and movement introduced me to people I wanted to be like. Philip replies the next day, quickly and kindly. He writes that the songs we often return to as adults typically come from later than childhood, but tougher circumstances might mean that songs from further back take on a deeper significance. 'As to what it was about that song that affected you so strongly, I certainly couldn't say without knowing it, and could only guess even then. One might say simply – which is not to say trivially, it's important – that repetition of a known quantity offered a sense of control and predictability at a time of rupture and loss of external control. I'd guess too that there might have been an element of the music creating a channel for feelings that couldn't be articulated: the idea of "music sounding how emotions feel".'

Songs could appear holy to us when we needed them to be, he continues. 'At root, this is perhaps the same function of music as when it's used in sacred contexts, where it seems able to express what is otherwise ineffable. And this, I think, is not just because of the way the textures of music can be imitative of emotions . . . but also because the analogies between musical and linguistic structure persuade us that music is expressing something, even while it has no semantic meaning that we can articulate.'

At any rate, he writes, if this is even close to the truth, 'it reflects one of the reasons why music is so important, personally and culturally, because it can express things that are beyond words'. Melodies can sing by themselves and send messages to us. We respond to them, try to decipher them, our ears motoring those messages inwards.

*

I also came to love Wham! because of their videos. This was the mid-eighties, when the pop business was on an upward, skyrocketing curve. Record labels were becoming gargantuan. MTV was reconfiguring the pop TV market. A band's visual aesthetic was becoming as important as the music itself, as was the way that moving images were being used to sell songs.

The eyes of younger, more malleable audiences were also becoming easier to snag. Pop stars who could be role models became canny acquisitions. In the year of Wham!'s trip to China, Daniel Dotter of the University of Tennessee at Martin wrote an essay about this phenomenon: 'Growing up is hard to do: Rock and roll performers as cultural heroes'. Rock and roll pioneers had been anti-heroes in mainstream society, he said, before these qualities 'became more accept-able, even institutionalised' thanks to the commercial via-bility of their music. Consider how quickly the outrageous, hip-swinging Elvis Presley and those quick-witted longhairs, The Beatles, became folded into quotidian culture.

By the eighties, technology was also accelerating the impact of the hero, speeding up the 'sociocultural symbol-creation process', and transmitting him to broader audiences (it was usually a him in those days, although there were a few notable exceptions, like the invasive, disruptive Madonna, pop's glorious new Boadicea). 'For most of human history, cultural hero-systems have been created and maintained through relatively inefficient modes of communication,' Dotter added. 'These have included folk and oral history, as well as the written word. In this social milieu the hero seems to emerge in the natural course of events – from the often repeated, expanded, and enhanced cultural myths of yesterday, of epochs ago.'

But times had rapidly changed, and while the speed at which heroes were created didn't dilute the idea of who they were, the delivery system by which they could be created and intensified had gone global – especially with the advent of satellite broadcasting. Dotter quoted a passage from Pulitzer Prize-winning anthropologist Ernst Becker to underline his point. 'It does not matter whether the cultural hero-system is frankly magical, religious and primitive, or secular, scientific, and civilised. It is still a mythical hero-system in which people serve in order to earn a feeling of primary value, of cosmic specialness, of ultimate usefulness.'

In 1985, I wanted nothing more than to feel cosmically special and ultimately useful. I was also still pliable and fresh, like brightly coloured Play-Doh, and on the lookout for more gods to follow. I looked forward to weekends when I could watch pop stars popping on *No. 73* or *Saturday Superstore*, loving the four-minute mini-movies of them that would occasionally be shown, set to perky soundtracks.

One morning, there was an interview with a singer who used to be in a band called Adam and the Ants, and they showed the video to an old song of theirs, a retelling of the story of Cinderella. The effect of the sound on me was instant: it didn't sound pretty, like Wham!, but wild, feverish, anarchic. It began with the sound of men yelping to the thwack of a drum, before a melody kicked in, strummed and stark, followed by some uplifting key changes.

The video ran. It wasn't any regular retelling of a fairy tale. It was an update with a twist in its plaited tail. The twist was that Cinderella didn't have to wait for Prince Charming to save her. Cinderella was saved by being *turned into* Prince Charming. He was being adored by the masses. That's what I wanted to be.

*

When I became entranced with Adam Ant, I knew he was pretty, but I didn't want to marry him. I wanted to be him: a bold, audacious hero. Quickly, I incorporated him into the stories I wrote, in pastel-coloured exercise books brought home by my mother. She was back in work now, after Dad's death, as a primary school teacher, my little brother being looked after by my grandparents, who lived around the corner.

I made up stories about Adam going on adventures. Some stories would involve battles against George Michael (how quickly the attentions of young girls switch and shift). Adam's historical, New Romantic fashions were perfect ingredients for childhood fantasy. Here was a person turning the past into a fabulous, ostentatious cartoon — and a cartoon with

Adam in it would have been better than *The Pink Panther* or *The Flintstones*, which I watched in the early mornings on TV before my mother and brother woke up, around the revolving Ceefax and Oracle pages. (Adam and his friends were probably still up then anyway, I'd discover later, after the night before.)

Adam and the Ants were also a band from *my* past – when I was a toddler – which held a weird allure. They'd released 'Prince Charming' in September 1981 and split up a year later, so their narrative had ended for now; I was picking up the inky pen. I still don't know why the video was shown on TV all those years later. Maybe it was because Adam had just released his 1985 solo album *Vive Le Rock*, and they wanted to contrast his new style – in real life, in the studio – with his old one. Or perhaps it was to illustrate what a huge star he had been, to remind people who he was, if he had been forgotten.

I vaguely remember him wearing a black leather jacket in the studio in 1985, and no make-up, looking far more grown-up. I liked him much more in the video from 1981, being teased by his moustachioed sisters, then being struck by dazzling light from above by his fairy godmother, the British actor Diana Dors. I loved her too, how she arrived in the clouds before being beamed down to earth. She looked round and cosy, radiantly raising her wand. I loved her turning the toy car Adam was playing with into a full-sized convertible, in lieu of a carriage. Then she turned an ordinary pretty boy into royalty.

This was a better Cinderella story than the one I had read in my bedroom. I had a set of slim Ladybird hardback fairy tale books, decorated lavishly with images from paintings. My collection included *Snow White and Rose Red*, the story of two sisters living with their widowed mother, in which Rose Red's liveliness was seen as inferior to Snow White's sugar-sweet shyness and quietness, and *The Princess and the Pea*, the story of a girl seen to be a suitable bride because she felt a small green vegetable as she slept through a mountain of mattresses. I never liked these books, but back then I didn't know why. I know now they were telling me that delicacy and daintiness were virtues to aim for. At seven, and still at forty-three, I possess neither.

But Adam rewrote the rules. When he was dressed in Cinderella rags, he looked mildly annoyed by his sisters, but not utterly crestfallen. He also had friends around him, urging him on. As Cinderella on parade, he looked completely in command. He made his peers gaze up at his magnificence, but then he also emerged in their midst, led them in a dance.

Most importantly, the Cinderella I'd read about before was searching for a Prince Charming to validate her. Adam wasn't looking for anyone to validate anything. He was grabbing the chandelier himself, dictating the new rules of the room. I wanted to be the mirror image of him, grab the fittings with my own little hands.

*

I didn't know back then that Adam storyboarded the video and directed it with his bandmate Marco Pirroni. When I found out as an adult, I thought, wow, how fantastic: he was literally in charge of his character's story arc. It's still a great video, too, an ambitious DIY affair full of drag-fuelled pantomime charm and awkward punkish edges.

'Prince Charming' is also important to me because it's the first song I remember where I paid proper attention to the words. Respect yourself and all the people around you, Adam told me. Don't lower yourself and disregard all your standards. And don't you ever – don't you ever – stop being dandy. The repetition felt defiant. Kids weren't often told stuff like this. Delivered by Adam, this direction felt naughty but direct. The feral yowls that started the song let me scream.

I also got into dressing up at this age, playing a game called 'Fashion Show' with my mother and grandma on weekends. I'd rummage through Grandma's wardrobe – a profusion of accessories ready for concerts and chapel – and try on her hats, berets, pearls, brooches and high heels. I enjoyed being someone who definitely wasn't me, even when I couldn't walk properly down the hall from the stairs towards the living room and the radiogram.

Watching the 'Prince Charming' video now, there are references I would have never understood when I was small. After Adam swings on the chandelier, he doesn't lose his glass slipper. Instead, he smashes a glass ceiling, ferociously, cathartically, then starts to take on other guises: he becomes The Man With No Name from *The Good, the Bad and the Ugly*, Rudolph Valentino from *The Sheik*, Vito Corleone from *The Godfather* and, bizarrely, Alice Cooper. Of course, he had changed himself before when he became Adam Ant.

His intense 2006 autobiography *Stand & Deliver* – named after the single that preceded 'Prince Charming' – begins at this moment. 'Adam Ant was born in 1976, in the grey, cold echoing emergency ward of Friern Barnet Hospital, North London. He was smacked into consciousness by a hard-faced and overworked charge nurse, who calmly said, "Wake up you little bastard.'"

Adam then writes that he had killed Stuart Goddard, the name he was born with in 1954. 'A handful of my mother-in-law's pills taken from the yellow cabinet in her bathroom had done the job.'

Stand & Deliver goes into detail about his tough life. As a child, his father was violent, regularly beating up his mother. When Adam was seven, his parents separated, or rather '[Dad] just didn't come home anymore.' Sharing a room in a council flat near London's Regent's Park with his mum, she had to work all hours as her ex-husband rarely paid maintenance. The young Stuart then passed the eleven-plus to go to grammar school and became even lonelier, leaving most of his friends behind.

The thing that soothed him was television – 'I never argued with it. Whatever it had to offer suited me fine' – and then his mum got a job up the road in St John's Wood, working as a housekeeper for Paul McCartney. Adam often went with her after school to McCartney's huge Georgian house, seeing his Höfner violin bass, his collection of psychedelically painted instruments, and boxes of gold and silver discs. He also walked McCartney's sheepdog, Martha, and was given a copy of The Beatles' LP *Revolver* by McCartney's assistant before it was released.

In his late teens, Adam went to art school and had a breakdown. It came suddenly: he couldn't cope with his life, and felt he needed to wipe the slate clean. He renamed himself Adam Ant after his three months in the psychiatric ward, he explained to BBC 6 Music's Matt Everitt in 2011, and he chose it because 'Adam was the first man' and Ant 'because if there's a nuclear explosion, the ants will survive'.

He pointed out he wasn't weird for doing this. 'I don't think it's that surprising. Sting changed his name, Cliff Richard changed his name. Lots of musicians do it.' Pop is driven by such transformations.

Adam and the Ants were born a year after that. *Prince Charming* came three albums into their lifespan, after the fetish-inspired, post-punk *Dirk Wears White Sox* and their caterwauling, fantastic pop breakthrough, *Kings of the Wild Frontier*. Later I met other fans who'd watched his body arc on that chandelier, swinging in a way he wasn't meant to, and felt its momentum ricochet deep inside them. We were all sitting in our living rooms yearning to be propelled forward, wanting people to admire how bravely we were all holding on.

*

In 2015, two psychologists at the University of Richmond, Virginia, Scott T. Allison and George R. Goethals, wrote a paper called 'Hero Worship: The elevation of the human spirit'. It proposed to change the way in which heroes and hero narratives were ignored in contemporary psychology. Hero narratives, they argued – the likes of which had been debated in literary theory for years, from Joseph Campbell onwards – were 'highly effective delivery systems for imparting complex truths and for elevating humans toward a higher emotional and behavioural state'. Stirring narrative accounts of heroic deeds were the fuel for both 'human survival and for human thriving', and stories of heroic action could also impart wisdom by supplying 'mental models, or scripts, for how one could or should lead one's life'.

Allison and Goethals also argued that heroism was based on a person's needs, and that it was always in motion: our ideas of it would change depending on what was going on in our lives. Heroic stories also served two functions, an 'epistemic' one and an 'energising' one. By epistemic, they meant that hero stories imparted knowledge and wisdom to the people that needed them. Its energising function related to these stories elevating people to believe that they were capable of positive action.

These theories sounded a little extravagant to me, a little bombastic, but they also resonated; I knew how much my heroes had helped me when I was little, after all. I also liked how Allison and Goethals described historical heroic stories as placing kids in 'a sense of deep time' – where young people can suddenly understand that the world has a past, a present and a future. My viewing of the 'Prince Charming' video had comforted me because it was a song from my past, but it had lingered with me in its afterlife, too. It was also a song from my father's present, and it was something he might have heard as a pop fan. The fact it had existed when he did, in all its silliness and extravagance, made me happy. It was also a song that would always exist in this form – three minutes and eighteen seconds of animated, frenzied adventure – with the potential to go on to create multiple legacies.

Heroic stories, Allison and Goethals concluded, also had the power to 'heal our psychic wounds'. This wounding emerged in 'countless stories . . . of ugly ducklings, Cinderellas, and other underdogs who through magic or the help of a deity turn their wounds into triumph. Heroes use their wounds to transform themselves and to redeem the world.'

As messages go, few could have been more powerful for me when I was seven.

*

In June 2011, I saw my prince for myself, in the most unexpected circumstances. I was at the London Palladium, reviewing a Tony Bennett concert; I had interviewed Tony earlier in the day, and he had written a note for my Aunty Velma, our neighbour in my childhood, who had looked after me during Dad's funeral, and at other times after my father died. 'To Velma, a pleasure', it said, in his quivery handwriting. It sat on her mantelpiece for the next eight years, and was still there when she died, at the age of ninety-three.

On that night, Tony had not long turned eighty-five, and was scampering around the stage, singing spryly. He revisited his past on songs like 'I Wanna Be Around' and 'Sing You Sinners', singing about revenge and how 'the devil kicks'. 'Moments remind us of a very different Tony who has long faded in memory – the washed-up drug addict of the 1970s,' I wrote in my review. Yet another artist had transformed himself entirely.

After the gig, there was an after-show party downstairs in the basement bar. At such events, critics pretend they're assembling to bag free glasses of wine, but many, like me, can't stop nosing to see if anyone famous will turn up.

I squeezed into a big, shambolic group in the corner that included a few familiar faces, among them my fellow Welsh broadsheet critic Simon Price, who had brought along a shy friend, tucked into the corner, wearing a hat. I spent the half-hour gabbing to a journalist at *The Times*, turning around every now and then to see if Tony had magically appeared, but not tonight.

As I was leaving, I turned towards Simon to say goodbye, and suddenly saw who his friend was, beneath the hat. He didn't have slashes of paint on his cheek any more, and the years had wound on, but that face had been etched in my mind for so long. I couldn't speak – and then he smiled – and I smiled back, a proper fangirl gurn. Then I ran away up the stairs, and at gone eleven on a school night, when most people were in bed, called my mother to tell her who I'd seen. She laughed, said that was great, asked me about Tony Bennett, then let me go, so she could let her daft daughter get her train, and finally get herself to sleep.

I find it funny that I had wanted to tell her. Adam wasn't an interest I'd talked to her about as a child – I kept my stories about him to myself – but he was another presence in my childhood that had suddenly made a comeback. He was a person filling an absence. It was a miraculous return. I've not seen him since, or gone to his gigs. I like to keep him in my memory in that moment, like a fabulous mirage.

But in the real world, he kept on performing and playing. Two years after that night, he released a new album with a brilliant, extravagant title: *Adam Ant Is the Blueblack Hussar in Marrying the Gunner's Daughter*. The Blueblack Hussar was his old dandy highwayman persona from 1981, brought back to life, and he has toured often since then, reconnecting with the people who had felt his influence within them. I'd like him to know now that he alerted a sad, anxious child to the best place from which the rest of her childhood could grow: the boundless, sacred empire of my imagination. Adam allowed me to yowl, smash through the glass and start writing my own stories. Many of which, back then, included meeting him. Dreams can come true.

Track 4

Buffalo Stance – Neneh Cherry

How Music Feeds Self-Expression

At ten, I found a new gang. They existed within glossy, messy pages and took shape in swirling headlines, tiny letters and exclamation marks stretching themselves into the margins.

By January 1989, things were quickly changing in my life. My mother had a new boyfriend, Glyn, whom she'd known since her childhood. In a few months, they were getting married. I still glow at the memory of a weekend away to Aberystwyth, when Glyn took me for a walk to the Royal Pier at dusk, where the starlings whirl in to find solace every evening in the foam from the waves. Here, my new dad asked my permission to marry my mam. What a sweet thing that was to do. I was being treated like a grown-up as I inched towards adolescence, and I liked it.

I was also five months into a new obsession that was helping me with this transition between old and new lives. It began the previous August, when I walked into Morgan's Newsagents in Gorseinon, the tiny town next to my village, and found something in the magazine racks that suddenly burst out of them, like a rainbow. It lifted me above the red-tops, the black and blue biros, the duplicate receipt books, the faded toys on the carousels, the sun-blasted birthday cards, the old boxes of penny sweets. I never missed the sweets after that visit, because I always went back to the shop with fifty pence every fortnight, returning with *Smash Hits*, which cost forty-eight, and two sugared mice in a striped paper bag.

Smash Hits became my tweenage Baedeker, a dense, lively guide to the universe of pop music. I have the first issue I ever bought, with Brother Beyond on the cover, holding skateboards. It is gloriously silly. It has a column on the Pat Benatar phenomenon ('She is a foxtress, a rockstress, a socktress – i.e. she has very nice foot garments – and a lockstress – i.e. she has very nice hair'). It has an introduction to Tanita Tikaram. ('Does she know what so-called "house music" is? "Yeah, it's music they play in a house, isn't it?" Oh dear.') It has a quiz about pop stars' interesting scars, a crap joke corner, and a weekly fact box to cut out and keep. This issue's featured artist was Billy Idol: 'Sir Billiam once went swimming in Majorca with his leather trousers on and ruined them,' we're told.

Smash Hits was frivolous and ridiculous, but it was also sweetly rebellious, refusing to put pop stars on a platform. It didn't faint at their feet, but fleshed them out as real, awkward people. This approach often made *Smash Hits* slyly political. I found out about Section 28 from an interview with the Pet Shop Boys, the next boys after Adam Ant, alongside a-ha, to win my beating heart. Pop stars were often asked about meaty subjects. On nuclear disarmament, for instance, Sade was pro, Gary Numan was not. On the Royal Family, Mick Jones, then in Big Audio Dynamite, said, 'I'm afraid I'm all for them.' What would these artists do if they were Prime Minister? Mark E. Smith: 'Halve the price of cigarettes, double the tax on health food, then I'd declare war on France.'

Crucially, girls played a huge part in this universe, regularly springing and grinning out of its double-page spreads. I didn't realise how wonderful this was at the time, or how inured I would become to women looking stern, pained or bored on fashion and style magazine covers barely a decade later. In some areas of the media today, things have changed dramatically, but when music monthlies put women on the covers it still feels like a miracle. Let's not forget the bulk of their content is still about men, and still largely written by men.

But back on 11 January 1989, a girl I'd recently fallen in love with, much more than the others, had her first *Smash Hits* cover. I'd seen her on *Top of the Pops* just before Christmas, which I was now allowed to stay up late to watch, wishing I was there in the studio, tasting clouds of dry ice on my tongue. She arrived between two other women I already loved: Kim Wilde, singing about love being a 'Four Letter Word' in a black forties dress, and Kylie Minogue, in a waistcoat, performing her new single, 'Especially for You', with Jason Donovan, extolling the virtues of rapprochement after heartache.

I loved those songs, and still do, but this new girl was different. She bounced onto the screen wearing a gold bra, gold medallion, gold bomber jacket and a black, lycra stretchy skirt, pulled tight over her belly. One minute: that belly clearly contained a baby. And she was dancing – her arms to the sides, in the air, in her hair – to these sharp, relentless rhythms, her eyes searching, her smile infectious, singing the chorus like everything depended on it. And on the verses, hard and fast – what was this? – Neneh Cherry was rapping.

*

'I just remember how positive it was. She was a positive *person*, wasn't she? And she was rapping in a British accent, and before that, British rap was shit for a long time. This wasn't shit!'

When I was ten, I looked up to one writer more than anyone else: Miranda Sawyer. I remember seeing her byline picture, her short bleached blonde crop, her big grin. Over three decades later, she's on the phone to me from her flat in South London, full of vitality and generosity on a winter's afternoon. 'Then I noticed, ooh, she's pregnant. She's pregnant! That felt brilliant too. Her doing these brilliant raps and dancing, like that adage about doing it backwards in high heels, but better.'

I first met Miranda a few months into my first music journalism job in 2003. She was fun, down-to-earth and generous, just as I'd hoped. In January 1989, she was a few months into her job at *Smash Hits* and also in her first stint as a music writer. She'd applied the previous summer while doing a job cleaning university rooms near London's Old Street – a job she took, she says, because it threw accommodation into the deal. She tells me she stuck pictures from magazines on her wall to cheer the room up, including one from Neneh Cherry's first interview with *The Face* magazine.

A few weeks later, Miranda was in *Smash Hits* HQ, being asked in her interview who she'd put on the cover. She said Brother Beyond and her editor liked her suggestion: it turns out her first issue was mine too. *Smash Hits* HQ was full of young women, and she describes them in lively detail. There was art director Jaqui Doyle – 'all long hair, baggy West London raver clothes and big trainers' – cramming jokes and pictures into every corner, making the magazine feel like a fabulous playground. Then there was senior staff writer Sylvia Patterson, the interviewer never spoken in the same breath as Lester Bangs and Nick Kent while being their non-sneery significant superior, smoking all the time in gothy, voluminous shirts. 'She was also not a stranger to a crimper back then,' Miranda adds.

On the masthead of our first issue, I also find Naomi Davies, Harriet Dell, Josephine Collins, Lola Borg, Julie Horton and Alex Kadis in Editorial. There's only one junior man in the advertising department, surrounded by Sandra McClean, Margaret Leonard, Lucy Gallagher and Sally Cokell. Features Editor Derrin Schlesinger is now a film and TV producer (*Four Lions, Nathan Barley* and *The IT Crowd* are on her CV), while *Smash Hits'* publisher was a woman too, unusually for that time. Mary Calderwood is now an executive producer in music videos, and won a Grammy in 2011 for her work with Adele.

All the women at *Smash Hits* could follow the beat of their own drum, 'and later I discovered how unusual that is,' Miranda says. 'If women are in an immensely female environment, especially in a magazine environment, there can be a tendency to move as one. I mean, I had a friend who worked for *Vogue* who within four weeks had started thinking £1,000 was a decent price for a skirt. It was fucking mad! But at *Smash Hits*, it wasn't like that. What was important was "what pop music do you like" and you could like Kylie or the Beastie Boys or Bon Jovi or whoever. You could like anyone and be anyone, and that was great for girls.'

I have other old issues of *Smash Hits* that I've picked up from eBay and obscure pop culture sites online. Women from all genres, ages and places fill these issues: I flick through another in front of me while I'm on the phone, and find Yazz, Tiffany, Gloria Estefan, Carol Decker, Adeva, Enya. No woman was ever sexualised, I say to Miranda. Was that a choice? 'Oh, absolutely. We had a duty of care.

If an artist was seen as sexy, we might acknowledge that by calling her a kind of "pervstress" but that was that. We didn't want women being sexualised. It made me feel upset and uncomfortable too.'

Miranda talks about how sexist popular culture was in the late eighties, and about Page Three's ubiquity; she recalls how inured we all were to silent, gleaming women framing men centre-stage on popular game shows. I suddenly remember sitting in a local car garage with my grandfather after school when I must have been eight or nine, the wall behind me plastered with pictures from tabloid newspapers I knew of women with big hair and bigger breasts. I still know their names now, as I did then, which shows how well-known and accepted they were: Linda, Samantha, Maria, Kathy, Suzanne.

But in pop, women weren't static and exposed. They were creative and playful, and their sexuality was secondary to their talent, whatever they looked like. 'Think of Yazz! She is gorgeous – she was a model – but she wasn't slinking about. She was: "We're going to dance now and this is going to be brilliant."'

When Miranda did her first column reviewing singles for *Smash Hits* in November 1988, 'Buffalo Stance' was in the postbag. She instantly loved it. She acknowledged a version of the tune had been kicking around for a while, first released in 1987 as the B-side to 'Looking Good Diving with the Wild Bunch', a single by the male duo Morgan McVey: Morgan was Jamie Morgan, a model and photographer, McVey was Neneh's boyfriend and later husband and manager, Cameron McVey. Bomb The Bass's Tim Simenon had remixed the track – untangled it, rewired it – given it fresh, neon-lit energy. Miranda called it 'the best dance record in yonks' and made it runner-up single of the fortnight (only because the Pet Shop Boys had the cheek to release their greatest ever song, 'Left to My Own Devices', in the same week). The *Smash Hits* team read Miranda's review and decided to give Neneh a cover. 'I remember thinking, "Oh, I'm chuffed. I made them notice her!"'

We discuss why Neneh's performance on *Top of the Pops* might have had such a big effect on people like me – young girls noticing adulthood on the horizon, teetering on the edge of puberty. 'I reckon what you're wanting at that age is a sense of freedom and a sense of identity, and pop music offers you that in a really small package, doesn't it? I mean, a piece of music can absolutely take you to a place that you know exists, and you know you'll get there eventually. But you can't drive, go out, drink, have sex – well, maybe you could, but all these things are not that great for you at that age – so to have it offered to you in pop music in that safe way, for you to experience that kind of rush, is everything.'

Essentially, pop music offers *another* way for young girls to feel a rush in their lives, Miranda adds, and I realise why I loved her so much as a ten-year-old. She was like a knowledgeable, street-smart big sister back then. Even better, she still is. 'And it's really important to feel that rush in your life. Because otherwise, well, you'll just walk through it like a zombie, won't you?'

She now has a ten-year-old daughter – the same age I was when I saw Neneh. We discuss how young girls these days, in our separate experiences through family and friends, are much bolder than we were; we glory at how much positive progress there has been. But Miranda's still keen to point out how tough things can get. 'You're still being constantly rated on a fanciable chart when you walk into a room, even by other girls, and it's awful. But in pop music, the rules are different. It's less about what you look like than how you're delivering this line.'

In pop, you don't have to be Mariah Carey, she goes on. 'You can be somebody like Madonna, who isn't the best singer, but she's a real rock star. In our day, you could be like Neil Tennant, and have an identity that is singular and a bit odd, but has a charisma that will make it through. Experiencing these people helps you access new identities, doesn't it?' Yes, it does. 'And better still, all these things go direct to the heart.'

In Neneh's first *Smash Hits* cover interview, she sounds different to other pop stars, thoughtful and wise, older than her years. She talks about being worried for Bros ('You can kind of imagine the blows and the unhappiness that those guys might experience in the next few years'). She talks about getting involved in 'girlie catfights' when she was ten and cussing drunk men for touching her bottom at Glasgow Airport ('They were pathetic!').

She also hopes that 'Buffalo Stance' inspires young people. 'To make up their own little raps and stuff. Get out and do it, kids! You don't have to be a great musician to make great records.' Her advice was straightforward, accessible, animated. 'You just have to have a lot of good ideas.'

*

In January 1989, puberty was dragging me through the contortions and confusions of my last year in primary school. I was already the five foot seven I'd remain, a reluctant owner of a training bra, and my periods would begin before the year was out. I looked a little like an adult but didn't feel like one at all, especially around my shorter, smaller peers. I desperately wanted to articulate myself properly too, to make everything make sense.

At home, I didn't yet listen to my favourite music much. I didn't have a Walkman, and felt awkward asking to borrow Dad's old headphones, go over to the hi-fi, and sit on the carpet to listen to the few albums that I had, by Five Star or The Bangles. The radio wasn't on regular rotation as it was at Grandma and Grandpa's either; our home's soundtrack was the songs Mam would play on the piano. These were hymns, Welsh folk tunes and soft traditional songs, things for the children to sing along to at school; she had also become a chapel organist and accompanist for the village choir. This music felt comforting to hear through the house, but leagues away from the pop that I loved.

Mam had also started taking Jon and me to our local Welsh chapel. The best thing about the experience for me was the singing: working out harmonies around dense Welsh words which I didn't really understand, wrapping my tongue around rolling Rs and airy double-Ls, playing with the rhythms of a peculiar language. In Wales, hymns are sung communally and without ornamentation, unlike the gospel that flows through America or the Gaelic psalms that eddy through the Hebrides. You have to come together with other people to form a mass of consistent sound, an approach to harmony that matches the spiritual principles of the Welsh Baptist tradition. Everyone stands together in a song. Nobody stands out.

When I saw Neneh, she was playing with the rhythms of language in a very different setting. Her means of delivery was distinctive. She wasn't hidden in a group. She had the confidence to do something I liked while being out front and raising her voice.

I also loved 'Buffalo Stance' because it was a whirligig, free-flowing patchwork of ideas I didn't understand: four minutes full of peculiar phrases, people and street scenes. I had no idea what a buffalo stance was, but I guessed it was about attitude (Cherry told the *New York Times* in 1989 it was 'an attitude you have to have to get by – it's not about fashion but survival in inner cities and elsewhere'). The Buffalo crew were a group of photographers, artists, musicians and models redefining the British look through multicultural influences and street style – I didn't know about that either, nor would I until I started reading *The Face* in my late teens. I did love Cherry's style, though, and dreamed I could channel it, although hooped earrings and Betty Boop T-shirts back then, bought by my mother, was as far as I went.

I didn't understand a lot of the lyrics. A man putting a girl on a corner so he could make a pile: back then, no idea. Equally mystifying was the idea of what a gigolo was. I just liked saying the word, my tongue moving from the top of my mouth, my lips circling each syllable. But I liked the unusual portraits that leapt out of Neneh's mouth, and how her lyrics seemed to paint these characters as rounded people: the person with crocodile feet and his hands in his pockets, the nasty-curled girls sucking bottled beer through straws. Neneh used turns of phrase that wouldn't have felt out of place on Saturday night sitcoms or soap operas, which gave me an entry point into this world. Her accent stirred big dollops of Britishness into the mix too, giving me a hand into unfamiliar territories.

I also hung onto the morals that emerged from 'Buffalo Stance'. Neneh told me that money should never win a person's love, that I should give someone I cared about something deeper in my soul. These were like the lessons of 'Prince Charming' but more grown-up and mature.

Then there were the questions in her lyrics, which I imagined being directed specifically at young girls like me, for us to respond to. Who's looking good today, Neneh sang. She was, and we were. What was he like? We agreed he was an idiot. You know what I mean? Huh! And somehow we did.

*

I tried to find out why Neneh's rapping moved me by researching its effects on young girls. A few recent studies by sociologists and psychologists leapt out. In 2016, Raphael Travis, Scott W. Bowman, Joshua Childs and Renee Villanueva of Texas State University published a paper called 'Musical Interactions: Girls who like and use rap music for empowerment'. Limited work had been done previously on the positive sides of rap, they explained; the genre's influence on risky behaviour among teenage girls had been studied much more often. Such is the way of the women-doubting world.

'A consistent theme among hip-hop's cultural values is the negotiation of identity and the contexts that shape identity,' Travis and his research team explained. 'Perspectives may vary widely as to whether an individual's efforts toward self-improvement are more helpful or harmful . . . but hip-hop culture also often offers a voice for youth developing an individual political consciousness, and organising among other youth for social and political change.'

They described how symbolic interactions with culture shape young people, too: how their engagement with ideas beyond their normal circumstances can positively shape their behaviour.

The team recruited 531 participants, 202 of them female, so that the girls wouldn't know that the study was targeted at them. Everyone was asked about the music they loved, and what they loved about it specifically. Travis and his team discovered that the women empowered by rap in their study went through a process of 'negotiation' while listening to rap lyrics: 'Females that engaged with the music construct a personal process that established an "I" and "me" connection to the empowering lyrics, allowing for an internal dialogue that facilitates identity construction. There is a clear process of seeking lyrical content that supports a positive, empowering internal dialogue.' The majority of the women also rejected lyrics and symbolic interactions that 'were non-supportive on a personal level'.

Another study in 2017, at the University of Amsterdam, focused on how rap could help regulate emotions in even younger people. Neuropsychologist Sylka Uhlig, alongside Erik Jansen and Erik Scherder, divided up a group of 199 pre-adolescents aged between eight and eleven. Half became a control group that continued with school life as normal. The others received thirteen classes of rap music therapy.

Over four months, the rap classes focused on three things: engaging the children with rhythm against an external beat; singing and rapping vocal sounds together to encourage the expression of feelings; and the learning of lyrics and rhymes, allowing the students space to contribute their own suggestions to the mix. The therapy group recorded unambiguous, significant improvements on measures related to emotion, hyperactivity and inattention in all pupils. A different register of speech gave these young people a new, thrilling foundation to build themselves upon.

The closest I got to rapping, predictably, was dreadful: trying to perform 'Buffalo Stance' in the playground, with a South Walian accent, with the friends I was starting to make. We had already started to bond after learning Bananarama's dance routines, including mastering the twirl in the chorus to 'I Want You Back' (which I can still do today, and last did in public at their reunion gig in 2017, alongside female friends from primary and comprehensive school, tertiary college and adult life). Rapping provided even better entertainment. We threw words out, mangled them, got them totally wrong, but kept trying our best. The energy of trying to inhabit an attitude as we experimented together felt brilliant. Our playground was our pop video soundstage, where no one was watching but us.

*

Years later, I interviewed Neneh about 'Buffalo Stance' and the impact it had for a feature about the album it came from, *Raw Like Sushi*. It was the fourth time I'd spoken to her out of five, a fact that still fills the ten-year-old girl inside me with bewilderment. 'Rap was freedom,' Neneh told me in December 2018, thirty years on from the *Top of the Pops* performance. 'With rap, you could find your own way within it, your own form of expression, and that felt like a big thing as a woman. There's something very powerful within rap, anyway. You're not dependent on the words working with the melody. You can just pour out what you really want to say in an unrestricted way.'

Neneh had a musical childhood that was almost the opposite to mine: itinerant, loose, international, free-form. Born in Stockholm in 1964, her mother was radical Swedish artist Moki Karlsson and her stepfather was jazz trumpeter Don Cherry, the main paternal figure in her life since she was a baby. Her father was Ahmadu Jah, a drummer whom she first met when she was eight. At fifteen, she spent three months with him in Nigeria, Ghana and then in his home country of Sierra Leone. She'd arrived as a young punk, but on the trip, she heard a griot for the first time, a West African troubadour telling stories of his tribe. 'I arrived in a Clash T-shirt and combat boots and when I left had forty-four braids and a lapa,' she laughed.

Many critics trace the roots of rap back to the idea of the griot. In her 1991 essay 'Rap Music: an education with a beat from the street', Catherine Tabb Powell of the University of the District of Columbia laid out how rap was not engineered by Tin Pan Alley, but everyday environments: '[Rap] is a homemade, street-level genre . . . part of a tradition of oral recitation started in Africa many centuries ago . . . griots would entertain and educate their audiences by reciting tribal history and current events . . . often embellished by satirical asides, proverbs, jokes, praise and ridicule.' Calypso and mento music in the Caribbean also took root from the griot tradition, she wrote, and rhythm was hugely important in the delivery of their stories.

Neneh told me she'd seen the influence of the griot in the spoken-word artists that emerged during the civil rights movement in the US, which was at its height when she was small; for several periods in her childhood and teenage years, she lived in New York. 'There's something in the speaking of words that helps change the conversation, you know? You see it in the power to record history and social commentary that came from people like the Last Poets, and performance poets like Jayne Cortez.' She then heard the roots of what became rap at the Queensbridge public housing development 'around 1977', just across the Hudson River from Manhattan – she had a boyfriend who lived there, and heard men advertising the sound systems that were about to play. 'It quickly became about these people introducing themselves, saying: "This is my name, my street, where I come from." This was long before freestyling, but it was interesting even then: it became about talking about who you were.'

The first female rap track that affected Neneh was 'Vicious Rap' by Tanya 'Sweet Tee' Winley in 1980 – a fantastic, accessible single by an artist whose father had released Malcolm X speeches on the same label. To a background wail of police sirens, it was one of the first examples of what some people called 'conscious rap': it railed at the government ('they sit back, relax and don't give a damn') and also spoke of the collective might of girls ('they put the dudes in check, and it ain't a joke').

By then, Neneh was sixteen, living in London, and a member of British all-female post-punk group The Slits, living in a squat with its main vocalist, Ari Up. 'As a record, it was raw – it felt like [Sweet Tee] had delivered her words in two takes, on fire. It had a quality like Aretha Franklin, or Patti Smith.' To Neneh, the track felt full of independence, with Sweet Tee having ownership of the space she was in as she was speaking. 'I guess as a young woman back then – and a woman throughout my life – when you hear a woman that's in the zone like that, it really hits you. And I hadn't really heard a lot of women sound like that.'

I knew what she meant.

Nine years later, Neneh, to ten-year-old me, was in the same zone. She'd been in a few bands after The Slits – Rip, Rig + Panic and Float Up CP – and had a baby in 1983, Naima, with her then-partner, Bruce Smith from the Pop Group. 'Buffalo Stance' emerged a few years later after Tim Simenon of Bomb The Bass got in touch, wanting to remix 'Looking Good Diving with the Wild Bunch'. Things happened naturally, organically. 'I never really sat down and thought, "Oh, I want to do the track like this,"' Neneh said. 'It was just, "OK, this is what we've got, this is who's there, let's do it." You'd get a beat together, write a few lyrics, wear some good clothes and just own it. What I was doing was from the heart but also a kind of fearless space.'

Within weeks of 'Buffalo Stance' coming out, it was heading up the charts. Then the *Top of the Pops* performance came along. Neneh admitted it felt like a monumental thing: 'But there's always been this side of me that has always felt a bit weird – "Do I fit in here, do I belong here?" But my response has always been, "Yeah, screw it. Let's just do this."' I hadn't thought of her as someone who ever felt she didn't fit in – she was an uber-woman to me. But then she told me about the racism and sexism she'd faced as a child and a teenager, especially with friends in Sweden, and I realised how thoughtless I'd been. 'So having that attitude as a coping mechanism – "Take it or leave it, if you don't like it, tough, this is how it is" – meant being pregnant actually helped. I wasn't going to hide it. Also, being a woman of colour, I just felt like, "I've got to just hold this – I don't know if it's going to work, but this is how it's going to be."'

From the start, Neneh was also conscious of 'the girly entrapments in this industry that I wasn't interested in being a part of' – and that pushed her on. 'Women were put in such a stereotypical box by record companies and labels, and I wanted to do something else. And people forget there've always been formidable women doing things differently, of course, but there are also all these nice girls writing lyrics about wanting babies, or how you left me, who are written about more, who are so often sexualised.'

She wanted to write about the things nice girls sang about too: 'Because life is what it is: it's sweet and it's bitter and it's hard and it's painful and you long for love, all that stuff. But I wanted to approach it from another place. I didn't want to be: "I'm sitting here waiting for you, where are you?" I wanted to be: "What the fuck?"'

*

'Buffalo Stance' was only the beginning of my love for Neneh. Soon after came her baby girl, Tyson, and her second single, 'Manchild', which is still my favourite song of hers. The video is wonderful, set at the edge of the sea, twisting the idea of home into a psychedelic, watery landscape: Naima, now six, is playing on a swing, laundry is blowing on a washing line on the sand, baby Tyson is cuddled in Mum's arms, and then Mum hands her over, rips a turbaned towel off her head, and starts rapping.

After that came 'Kisses on the Wind', a single about a girl who matures before other girls do. I remember it resonating with a particular intensity, because I felt physically different to my friends. Looking back, I also felt psychologically different, because I'd had to grow up very quickly, navigating my way around grief.

Neneh continued making pop in her own conscious way. I loved 1994's million-selling, multilingual 'Seven Seconds' with Youssou N'Dour, about the first moments of a child's life when they know nothing about the horrors of our world. I loved 'Woman' from 1996, about how women get erased, but are built to last. Neneh took a long break from mainstream music-making after that. In an *Irish Times* interview in 2016, she talked about her frustrations with fame in the nineties. 'I felt like I kept banging my head against limitations . . . the idea behind making "Buffalo Stance" and *Raw Like Sushi* wasn't to be famous. It was to change things and do things the way that we do them, always with an idea of activism or a kind of rebellion.'

By the 2000s, Neneh was nothing more than a happy memory to me, a bright light from a time when I was becoming a woman myself. And then there she was on the bill at the last Big Chill Festival in 2011, which I was reviewing for work: I watched her with three female friends, agog, and felt the energy of 'Buffalo Stance' pour out from the stage. A year later, I interviewed her about her first album in years, a collaboration with avant-garde collective The Thing, and she was intelligent and warm-hearted, talking about her surprising, inventive covers of songs by Suicide and the Stooges, as well as by her beloved father, Don.

That day, she also told me how her youngest daughter, Mabel, later to be a Brit Award-winning pop star, was born only four months after Don died. Stepfather and pregnant stepdaughter had spent his last weeks together. 'And two days before he died, he sat with his hands on my stomach,' she said. 'It was like he was sending his last energy into her. Sometimes I look at her and think, "I wish you could have met him." But you know, he's still there.' Her words made me think differently about so many things.

I met her again nine months later, at a big personal moment in my life, at the by:Larm music festival in Oslo. I had been asked to interview her onstage. I was also five weeks pregnant. Neneh seemed nervous, which surprised me when she looked so confident singing and rapping live, but perhaps without these registers, she felt untethered. Musical performance allowed people a different realm of expression, a framework on which they could strengthen their identity.

But the interview was a joy — it felt easy and fun — and after it, I was so glad, I told Neneh about my pregnancy. I remember thinking how desperately unprofessional this was, but also that I didn't care. She hugged me and I held her tight, desperate for her attitude, generosity and sensitivity to soak its way into my bones, whatever happened next.

The baby didn't make it, but Cherry's songs had long done good, hard work. They had shown me how I could be a woman in a robust, secure way when I was on the edges of adulthood, when I didn't want anyone to mess with me. They still do, and they pop up in my head often. I welcome them, letting them dig deep, and deeper, into my soul.

Track 5
Drive – R.E.M.

How Music Obsesses Us as Teenagers

I walked through Mayfair in London on a cold, sunny November afternoon, along the sides of grand, leafy squares, towards a man with whom I'd had a relationship since I was fourteen.

When I first saw him properly, he was gliding over a sea of hands, wearing a shirt, white and crumpled, open at the neck. I saw the pale skin at his throat and the wide, flattened plane of his stomach. His shorts casually revealed his thighs and his calves. His pale eyes, his perfect mouth, his gawky jaw, looked like they were all carved out of marble.

I watched him being passed around like a god then tossed in the air like a plaything.

We spent days together in my bedroom after that, my door closed, my heart open, him whispering feverish things into my little pierced ears. He told me I was wild. He told me I was his possession. I listened, determined to live my life as he told me to live it, full of joy and wonder. Every night, I imagined reaching out and seeing him fully formed at the end of my bed, reaching out his hand, holding it in mine, the two of us sinking through the sheets, the earth, the whole universe.

My heart felt too full that day in Mayfair, rising up from my chest, like it was almost in my throat, or raw and ripe in my mouth. I had barely slept for nerves. We were about to have twenty minutes together, just the two of us, in a hotel room, for the first time.

*

There's something intrinsically unhealthy about falling in love with a much older man when you're in secondary school. At that age, you're vulnerable, but you also feel invincible. Your every response, psychological, physical, sexual, is on high alert. You're bloodily, feverishly, desperately alive.

Mr Seaton, a history teacher at my comprehensive, had made the introductions. At wet break-times, my friends and I would beg to be allowed in his first-floor room at the back of the tower block. We loved Mr Seaton because he had a poster of Evan Dando on his cupboard door and he would play tapes while he tried to get on with his marking. One day, he played *Automatic for the People*. I pestered him to make me a copy until he did.

Over the summer holidays that year, I found myself at a strip-lit urban cathedral in Leicester while on holiday at my new uncle's house. The name of the megastore glared at me in big, knowing red letters. Inside Virgin, I went to R and found a small, jewelled box with a picture on the front of a thick, golden sea; I felt something inside me unravelling as I took it up to the till, my other hand gripping onto my pocket money tightly, anticipating what these coins could possibly provide in exchange.

I got back to my uncle's front room, closed the door, unwrapped *Out of Time* from its cellophane, and ceremonially slotted it into the Walkman I'd been bought a few Christmases earlier. Peter Buck's guitar strings sounded like spiritual sirens. Mike Mills' brilliant basslines held the songs upright and straightened my spine. Bill Berry's drums were unshowy and subtle, always in service of the song. Michael Stipe sang of fantasies flailing around, lonely deeps and hollows, barefoot, naked, on a maddening loop. His voice unfolded me like the concertina of cassette liner notes I held in my hands.

In my mid-teens, I pored over liner notes like ancient scrolls, and I especially loved the liner notes to *Out of Time*. The mysterious artwork on the front, covered by a yellow R.E.M. logo, was shown in full inside: I found out years later it was called *Yellow Seascape With Film and Wood Blocks*, made in 1988–9 by American artists and identical twins Mike & Doug Starn. The original suggests two doors that you can open, so you can take the handles in your fingers and comfortably enter the water. They made me want to open them, experience full immersion.

Inside the concertina, there was also a photograph by the brothers, of a plant, taken in black-and-white like a daguerreotype. There were others of fecund fruit and flowers and a cat's orange tail, struck by sunlight. There were also two cartoons, one featuring a man in a hat, looking like Michael, staring into the window of something that was called a sex theatre. The caption said: 'These faded, backlit transparencies remind passersby of the live spectacle happening inside.' I didn't want to understand what it meant, but also I did.

My fandom wasn't just about the delivery or the storytelling, I realised quickly: it was about something bigger, a band as a complete work of art. Not long after, I saw the video to their 1992 single 'Drive', filmed in stark black-and-white, the scene occasionally blasted by spotlights and lasers. Michael Stipe was crowd-surfing through a huge, pulsing audience, their hands raised to hold him, their fingers at full stretch, heated and hungry, their faces rapt. Sometimes, Michael looked numb, paralysed at the mercy of the mob. At others he looked ecstatic, his arms stretched out as if for a crucifix, blissfully accepting his fate.

It didn't sink in with me initially that the lyrics to 'Drive' were inspired by the idea of young people being politically mobilised. It was a song directed at American youth: youth that felt whacked out by a presidential term of George Bush after two terms of Reagan; youth that were fed up with being told what to do and where to go. 'Drive' was even used in a campaign to make voter registration easier in America, a 'drive' that later succeeded under Bill Clinton. I was more interested in the emotions in Michael's delivery than distant political machinations, in the way that he sang 'hey kids' like a mysterious invitation, like a breathy Pied Piper.

*

Years later, I'd find out that 'Drive' harked back to Michael Stipe's youth. 'Hey kids' was a line lifted directly from one of his favourite songs as a teenager, David Essex's peculiar, perfect dub-like 1973 debut, 'Rock On'. Michael talked about the effects of its weirdness on him in 2017, in an interview with NPR in the US, marking the twenty-fifth anniversary of *Automatic for the People*. '[It] just blasted right into the core of my being as a thirteen- and fourteen-year-old, I think, and presented to me this kind of set-up for what Patti Smith, CBGBs, Television, the punk rock scene in New York in 1974 and '75 would offer me. It was an entry into a universe that accepted me for who I was. I was already at that point where I realised that I was very different from all the kids around me . . . not eccentric, I never like that word.

But I was different.' 'Rock On' provided him with a key to a new door. 'A door that would open and never shut again.'

I used to watch 'Drive' on my own, on our video player, when I was meant to be doing my homework while my family were out. I had a baby brother now, James, a sweet, chatty toddler. Jon had just reached double figures and was getting into music too. Every Saturday, we'd sit and watch *The Chart Show* on ITV, taping songs that we liked, taping over others that hadn't held our interest after a few weeks. Given our different ages, the results were usually a hysterical mish-mash of sounds and styles, my nascent interest in indie buffering around videos by Lionel Richie, KWS, Mr Blobby.

I didn't want R.E.M. to be for my brothers' eyes, though. R.E.M. were exclusively for me. I'd wait until my parents would go out with the boys, hearing the car reversing up the drive on the way to the supermarket, to my grandma's, to Cubs, and I'd let the reels roll and sit motionless in front of the screen. Often, I would watch 'Drive' on repeat. It was a strange thing for me to keep watching, because I didn't like crowds. I found them claustrophobic, frightening – but this was one into which I could safely fold myself, imagine as a launchpad to future experiences, to test out the thrill.

The arrangement of the song built in intensity slowly, giving it a mood which was also slyly erotic. Halfway through the video, the crowd are blasted by a fire hose. The other band members stand in front of them, grinning, their instruments soaking wet. It's a knowing release.

The words Michael sang also added an element of flirta-tion into the mix. There is innuendo in the line 'What if you try to get off?' which I'm sure I didn't get at fourteen. I know I felt the word that followed it, though, an old trick out of rock and roll's playbook, one I already knew from songs by groups I'd loved a few years earlier, like Bros and New Kids On The Block. This time, the word carried a different weight in Michael's mouth.

'Baby,' he called me.

*

My love of Michael Stipe came in that peculiar period between worshipping saccharine boy bands and my GCSEs, when the teenage brain and body feel like they're aflame. Neuroscientist Catherine Loveday mentioned this stage of development when we spoke about our fathers. We often return to the music of our teenage years in tough times, she'd said, because this is when brains and bodies are developing at their quickest rate.

I Zoom her again, and she tells me this rapid development in adolescence is a relatively recent discovery in neuroscience. Twenty years ago, it was thought our brains stopped developing in mid-childhood. Now we know there are huge surges of development that come later, particularly in a network of structures colloquially known as the social brain. This includes the anterior cingulate cortex, a region important for understanding and empathising with people, and the fusiform face area, which helps us recognise faces and process the emotions they are exhibiting. As teenagers, we are drawn more to new faces and wanting to understand them, Loveday explains, even if they are just faces on a screen.

Parts of the brain's subcortical structure are also developing and maturing. The amygdala attributes meaning to the emotions we are feeling, while the nucleus accumbens acts as the brain's interface between our motivations and actions. Both have to communicate with the faraway prefrontal cortex, at the front of our brain, which is responsible for how we control our behaviour. 'These subcortical parts are about generating emotion, really a kind of unconstrained emotion, if you like – while the prefrontal cortex helps us to regulate what those emotion centres are doing.' Then Loveday introduces a theory in neuroscience called the mismatch hypothesis, which suggests that the prefrontal cortex can't keep up with the pace of the subcortical surges.

Loveday refers to the work of Sarah-Jayne Blackmore, a neuroscientist who wrote *Inventing Ourselves*, a book looking at different systems of the teenage brain. Blackmore's analogy is that the experience of having a teenage brain is like having a very fast car with lots of power, but no steering wheel: sensations of exhilaration and elation are everywhere, but without the tools to handle them properly, to rein oneself in.

The dopamine pathway that connects these subcortical areas to the prefrontal cortex is also developing quickly, speeding up the passage of feelings of pleasure. 'This pathway is really important for feelings of reward and obsessions,' Loveday says, 'obsessive love, and that kind of thing, which gives you an appetite, an active drive, to seek novelty.' The increased activation in this pathway is especially important in evolutionary terms: as they move towards adulthood, young people need to move away from their families to seek potential mates, and not have incestuous relationships. Another thing can also activate this pathway, Loveday says: 'It has also been shown to be activated by music.'

I think of myself in my bedroom, kicked into life by the rushing sounds of bright guitars, Michael Stipe's voice in my little speedy-head, telling me I've got to leave to find my way. The sensations back then were romantic and thrilling; I really felt like I loved him, that I wanted him to consume me completely.

Loveday then mentions another neuroscientist, Kim Lyall, who went into an fMRI scanner in 2011 to make herself orgasm, to see which parts of the brain were aroused. 'It's a study my students are always embarrassed by when I talk about it,' she says, with a smile. 'But when people have gone in MRI scanners to listen to their favourite songs, precisely the same areas are highly activated as Lyall's.' That dopamine pathway can also become triggered by people, so if you are experiencing that feeling in your brain while somebody is singing, then effectively they become associated with this kind of brain orgasm. There's also oxytocin being released, which gives a person a feeling of attachment and connection – but it can also shut someone off from other people who aren't in their blissful bubble. 'So what's going on in your mind is, wow, this piece of music is amazing, isn't that person fantastic – the brain is reacting as if you were actually close to that person and possibly even having sex with them.' She laughs. 'And yes – it can be quite over-whelming for people.'

I watch 'Drive' again at forty-three. I see other details. I see Peter Buck smiling as he's soaked, a fan's hand on his shoulder. On a few occasions, Michael looks at a fan and their eyes lock for a moment. Once he looks straight at the camera and sings at us. At me. I think about how fans and artists feed each other and seduce each other.

*

I look up Peter Care online, a filmmaker born in Cornwall who has long lived in LA, who directed the video to 'Drive'. His early work was experimental, with Cabaret Voltaire, Clock DVA and Killing Joke, before he bagged bigger jobs with Belinda Carlisle, Roy Orbison and Tina Turner. In 1991, he was working mainly in commercials, and had had enough; he called his friend Randy Skinner at Warner Brothers to see if she could give him something more meaningful. He tells me what happened next on the phone on a hot Californian afternoon, as I sink into the sofa on a warm British spring evening. 'I just couldn't do it any more – I said, I'll work for free if needs be, for any little tiny band with no money. And she said, well, have you heard of R.E.M.? And I was like, *what*?'

Peter knew them well. He had loved their early videos, and they'd just released a slicker proposition on screen that went on to win six MTV Video Awards. The video to 'Losing My Religion' helped propel them into the mainstream and did so without surrendering the band's commitment to weirdness. It referenced Caravaggio paintings, the art of Pierre et Gilles and a pivotal scene in Andrei Tarkovsky's film *The Sacrifice*, in which people in a room run from left to right past the camera and a milk jug shatters to the floor.

Peter signed up.

His first job with R.E.M. was 'Radio Song', and his video played around with ideas of the band's changing identity. The four members held up moving images of themselves, and were surrounded by others on TV screens; vintage film was mixed in that recalled their earlier, scratchier style.

Michael then invited Peter to lunch and asked if he'd be interested in making 'the greatest crowd-surfing video of all time'. He wanted to go shirtless, he added, and leant across the table, opening his buttons to show he'd already shaved his chest. 'He also wanted it to be out of sync,' Peter says, 'to look really off. "Peter – everything's off!"'

But the director was unsure about the idea of the front-man going bare-chested. 'And I'm surprised he didn't tell me to go fuck myself, but I said, it's going to look a bit like we're doing an Iggy Pop, and I don't think that's right.' He suggested Michael wear a white shirt instead, so the audience could see it getting wet. 'I said with a white shirt, there'd be a romance to it, a bit like the white sheets in *The Death of Marat*.' I look up this picture after our call: it's a famous painting by Jacques-Louis David of the murder of a French Revolutionary leader. There was another painting Peter had in his head too, by French Romantic painter Théodore Géricault, called *The Raft of the Medusa*. 'I said to Michael, it has a crowd with their hands up, a storm, water, and it's painted to look like the night with the stormy clouds, but it has a humanity to it.' The references were a bit over the top, he says, self-deprecatingly, 'but drama is something we gravitate towards when we're young, and Michael was up for it. And Michael was like, "OK! All right!"'

Peter's crew shot for two nights at the Sepulveda Dam, a three-mile-long feat of engineering near Los Angeles, constructed after the great floods of 1938, which killed over a hundred people. A radio call for R.E.M. fans saw hundreds turn up each night. A low-budget Lenny Arm crane was used to hold a camera and film everyone from above; it was wound loosely, creating a juddering effect, intensifying the strangeness with which Michael's hero-worship was being presented.

Peter did five more videos for R.E.M. after that, in which he explored the attention Michael received in more detail. In 'Man on the Moon', Michael looks like a movie star in a cowboy hat, doing Elvis impressions, jumping on trucks, confident and charismatic. In 'What's the Frequency, Kenneth?', he's suddenly reluctant: shot from the chin down, in rock star T-shirt and jeans. In 'Electrolite', he's filmed upside-down with plastic toy reindeer, in roller-skates, then pretending to be interviewed, then singing, hamming up his lip-syncing.

Peter emails me a few weeks after our phone conversation to offer more thoughts on capturing the feelings of the crowd in the 'Drive' video. 'I wanted the camera to focus on Michael like a fan would – all love, fascination, and no irony . . . I never thought the crowd were expressing adulation exactly. The people there were all big fans of R.E.M. of course, and Michael held them in the palm of his hand during the whole shoot. But like any mosh-pit, there was an energy beyond fandom, beyond what would normally be focused on the star on stage.'

To Peter in 1992, a mosh-pit ripe for crowd-surfing was more about the camaraderie within it, the shared experience it offered, and the job it had to do: 'i.e., don't drop the crowd-surfer,' he says. But then in 2001 he went to a pop video convention and saw 'Drive' on an enormous cinema screen for the first time. 'That was a revelation for me – magnified hugely, I saw faces in much more detail, their smiles, their anticipation in waiting for Michael to come their way . . . [they were] so much more powerful as a group of individuals.'

I used to imagine myself among them, my hands lifted up, as I sat on the living room carpet. From the vantage point of adulthood, I remember how isolating it felt back then being in my early teens. In the pre-internet age, I could only imagine being around people like those in the dam, all looking for a way to look up and grow up.

*

R.E.M. had a kaleidoscopic effect on my life. I filled notebooks trying to decipher Michael's murky poetry. I ordered band biographies from my local library (to the bemusement of the old woman who ran it), scouring pages for new rabbit holes I could disappear down. I spent all my pocket money from my after-school paper round on their back catalogue (their early albums had just been reissued by IRS: each cost £9.49, which was just short of two weeks' wages). I collected gig bootlegs in neon photocopied sleeves from early shows at the 40 Watt Club in Athens, Georgia, where R.E.M. were from, to their 1991 secret show at The Borderline in London, performing as Bingo Hand Job. These were £5 a time from the grimy record fairs in Swansea's Dolphin Hotel, next to the market that sold polystyrene pots of cockles and laverbread. Through R.E.M., I also found out about the photography of Man Ray, New Deal-era American murals, and the beauty of American train and street signage. I learned that music can be a starting point on a much broader cultural adventure, taking in the interests, heritage and history of people in a band, as well as wider influences from the immediate communities or countries they come from. I scavenged the back pages of *Melody Maker* for their video collections, which were particularly revelatory in this regard; these became the items I treasured most. My favourite short film of theirs was by Athens artist Jim Herbert, for the *Out of Time* album track 'Low', on their video anthology *This Film Is On*.

Based on an oil painting by American artist Elizabeth Jane Gardner Bouguereau, made in 1890, called *La Confidence*, it presented two young women sitting close together, one holding a letter and leaning in as if to whisper, with her other hand wrapped around the other girl's hair. On the original painting, this other girl is clasping her hands tightly together, but in the film they uncurl, and a butterfly flies out of her palm. Her friend reaches over and pulls a thread on her smock to untie it. A jug is picked up from the floor and its water poured over her feet: she moves them as if all her senses and responses have been stirred.

These close-up shots are of actors, but they look like the painting's subjects are breaking free of the canvas, gaining three dimensions. The meanings of the painting were being subverted, pulled apart, as I entered the frame.

In my thirties, I was reminded of the video to 'Low' when I found art critic John Berger's 1972 four-part series for the BBC, *Ways of Seeing*, on YouTube. This groundbreaking programme explored the work of philosopher Walter Benjamin, who had written earlier in the century about the mechanical reproduction of objects, including by photography and film, and how this had changed the nature, function and value of images in our lives.

Berger explained why Benjamin's work remained relevant to late twentieth-century society in accessible language, homing in on how 'false mystery and religiosity' now surrounded the ways in which we were told to appreciate art. This was done in the name of 'culture' and 'civilisation' in certain sections of society, he argued, but this worship of art was really about the cash value of original paintings, which had increased after images became easy to reproduce, and therefore easier to share and be seen.

'[But] I don't want to suggest that there is nothing left to experience before original works of art,' he added – a line that leapt out at me. 'A lot more is possible, but only if art is stripped of the false mystery and religiosity that surrounds it.'

By then, I'd found out that *La Confidence* had hung for years at a girls' school, the Lucy Cobb Institute, in Athens, Georgia. According to Kerry McNair of the Georgia Museum of Art, it was chosen to exact a 'moralising influence' on its pupils, presumably because of the girls' demure clothes and expressions. I thought about the painting I had come to know by other means, and how it existed far away from these pure intentions. 'Paintings are silent and still, and because their meanings are no longer attached to them,' Berger said in the first programme, 'they lend themselves to easy manipulation . . . used to make arguments or points which may be different, very different, from their original meaning.'

Berger said these new meanings could be positive and have huge creative potential: 'Images can be used like words. We can talk with them.' In the same episode, he also showed a painting of Jesus and two disciples by Caravaggio, *The Supper at Emmaus*, closing the camera in on different sections, playing opera behind the images, revealing how their meanings could be changed. Then he showed it to some

London schoolchildren, who instinctively understood much of its power: the emotion and action in the gestures of the subjects, the androgyny of the main character, that he could be someone holy.

Academics can make paintings seem inaccessible by describing them in complicated sentences, Berger told us, but very often, their power is easy to access. He showed me that young people could infer some of their deeper messages straightaway. He reminded me of a young girl poring over pictures in liner notes, on album sleeves, replaying 'Drive', and being pointed towards bigger, richer ideas, even if she didn't understand their every nuance. The curiosity they engendered in me was what mattered. It still is.

*

In the years that followed my R.E.M. epiphany, I fell in love with other acts whose use of art and photography also drew me into their music. In the corner of a second-hand shop in Llanelli's Stepney Arcade, I was enticed by an image of Alain Delon lying down, cast in green, on the cover of The Smiths' album *The Queen Is Dead*. The Smiths then introduced me to Keats, Yeats, Wilde and kitchen-sink films to the spectacular backdrop of Johnny Marr's guitars. After I saw thin light falling on sepia flesh on the cover of Suede's *Dog Man Star* in Sullivan's record shop in Gorseinon, their lyrics introduced me to the poetry of Byron and Blake; the doleful eyes of the old fisherman on the cover of The Cure's *Staring at the Sea* CD anthology led me to Penelope Farmer's extraordinary novel *Charlotte Sometimes*, which they'd written about for a single of the same name. I also responded

to the big, blue, abstract 3 on New Order's 1994 *Best of*, full
of a bright, calm modernity, and to the black-and-white
mausoleum on Joy Division's *Closer* – not knowing, when I
bought them both, within the space of a few months, that
these very different-looking bands shared three members.
They also introduced me to J. G. Ballard, Werner Herzog,
Futurism and Constructivism, as well as modernists and
post-modernists in art. I was drawn to bands whose work
valued design as much as sound, and my bedroom soon
became a gallery. My office at home, years later, still is, its
walls a tribute to record labels like Ghost Box, Factory and
Heavenly, all labels with clear, compelling aesthetics. My
door is covered with adverts for Hacienda club nights, which
I never attended, because I was still in primary school.

In my first year at university, I read the early work of
sociologist Angela McRobbie, who christened the concept of
'bedroom culture' in the seventies, validating the creativity
of many teenage girls. Teenage girls were encouraged to go
out less by their families, she wrote, because parents worried
about the risks presented to them by the outside world.
They were also encouraged to stay in the domestic sphere.
Bedrooms therefore became sites of rebellion, where girls
could create frantic patchworks of fandom, and mess around
with ideas of themselves.

My parents didn't mind me going out, but in my mid-
teens I often wanted to stay in. I layered postcards and
artwork all over my walls, creating a giant paper patchwork
over the B&Q magnolia. I was also sticking up faces, of
course, faces that sang to me on screens, faces that made
my connection to music human, faces that I stared at like a
baby, trying to understand the new realms they represented.

I wonder whether a reappropriation of images, by zealous fans, helps them further idolise the people they love. Perhaps the 'false mystery and religiosity' that Berger and Benjamin referred to gets transferred to pop star ephemera, to the fan club magazines and exclusive T-shirts I used to buy in the nineties, to the short-run pamphlets and limited edition coloured vinyl that rule the independent market today. These items also help cement people's distinctive identities, and give their obsessions longevity. They capture fleeting feelings in objects that can be used, re-used and returned to, if they're not just treated as window-dressing, objects that help us to remember, as we get older, how they made us who we are.

*

Fandom can also open up environments in which teenagers can be wildly creative, says Dr Lucy Bennett, a lecturer in media and culture at Cardiff University. We meet in autumn term in 2019, when she asks me to talk to her students about my music journalism career — I remind them I'm still a fan, just like they are. Bennett was born in South Wales, as was I, and is only a year older than me; instantly, we're rabbiting about the music we love and the venues we went to. She is also a huge fan of R.E.M., although she went a little further than me, literally, following them around Europe on their mid-2000s tours, and meeting them.

R.E.M. nourished and informed me as a teenager, I begin, gushing like Etna — all those references I'd collected, all those walls and notebooks I'd covered and filled — and that love felt productive and helpful during those tumultuous years.

She tells me about a fundamental text of fan studies, Henry Jenkins' *Textual Poachers* from 1992, which proposed that fans poach what they want from their idols, then rewrite their texts or produce meanings that are particular to their interests. 'Fans will home in on certain things that speak to them as individuals, and often write fan fiction, make songs or fan art – and that's great,' Bennett says. 'Jenkins' work represented fans as thoughtful critical thinkers for the first time, as creators, not hysterics.'

Bennett also mentions the work of media professor Cornel Sandvoss at the University of Huddersfield, and how he uses the concept of 'Heimat' – home – to describe what we're searching for as young fans. 'At that age, we're trying to find a new space, trying to work out our path, as we're about to go out into the world and work out who we are, and I think Heimat's a really useful concept in that sense, because music can offer a sense of home and belonging. At fourteen, fifteen, there's a sense that something is coming to an end, isn't there? You have friends at school, but that might change. You might be going to do A-Levels, and they might be going to work, or going to study elsewhere. You might not ever see them again. There's this really terrifying sense things are going to be very different, and music that speaks to you at that age just offers you a place to put those feelings. A bit of guidance around who you're going to be. You're just searching for where you belong.'

I ask Bennett what drew *her* to R.E.M. The idea of Athens, she says – this distant, romantic college town, far away from her home in the Welsh Valleys – and the emotional intelligence in the lyrics that she wasn't hearing in other music at the time. I say I felt the same. 'It's funny, isn't it?' She smiles. 'When you're that age, you think no one else will understand it, it's just about the connection *I* have with it. It's just become something special to *me*. And then later, you meet all these different people, like I'm meeting you, who love it – but when we were teenagers it was before any of us had the internet, and it was so hard to meet people. For so many of us, it wasn't possible.' Back then, fandom could feel very distancing. Today, we agree, it is often anything but.

We find out that we first saw R.E.M. live at the same time, in the summer of 1995 at Cardiff Arms Park. I confess to Bennett something terrible: that I found the experience disappointing. It was partly because I didn't love R.E.M.'s new album, *Monster*, which coloured the set-list and attitude of the show. It wasn't mysterious or slow-burning Americana. It was showy, brazen, obvious rock. It didn't offer me a space in which I could wallow; it was happy to exist without me.

But my disappointment was also about me having to share this band with other people. Lucy squeals in recognition. 'I did too! It was very private, very special to me, my love of R.E.M., and all of a sudden, I was in a huge music venue with all these thousands of people, many of whom were drunk, and weren't listening to the music, and I just got so frustrated. I said I'm never seeing them again.' But she did, in 2001, on Saturday morning show *CD:UK*, as one of only two hundred fans, after winning tickets through their fan club. She was also part of an R.E.M. online forum, Murmurs, at this point, through which she met fellow enthusiasts.

Soon, Bennett was joining her new community in the flesh, seeing her heroes live again, multiple times. On the mid-2000s tours, she regularly went backstage after shows and sometimes they even talked to the band, 'sometimes to Peter, about new music he liked, but not often – really, you were just there to chat to the other people'. She does remember one fan showing Peter Buck pictures of her bedroom, plastered with posters, and a horrible atmosphere of awkwardness emerging, him not knowing what to say. 'It felt odd, and as fans, you've got to act in the right way – but, you know, it's easy to say that. When someone and their art means so much to you, it's hard, because you get overwhelmed in the moment.'

*

Friday, 4 November 2011. I am sitting outside a hotel room in Mayfair, wearing a T-shirt I bought in Breaux Bridge, Louisiana, with my husband by my side, on our honeymoon back in May. I am wearing it for Michael – my favourite American Southerner – to notice it, to spot its strange, swampy design, to talk to me about it: to Jude the person, not Jude the professional.

Someone asks me a month later what was the best thing that happened to me in 2011. 'Meeting Michael Stipe!' I say, without hesitating. 'How about our wedding in April?' says my new husband. Eleven years on, he remains a saint.

The Connaught in Mayfair is a carefully chosen hotel, fancy but 'boutique', grand but not overbearing, as I assume the publicist thinks will befit R.E.M. All publicists work in these mysterious ways. R.E.M. are splitting up. They have decided they want to tell the press all about it, and I am here to do Michael Stipe's last ever online interview, for The

Quietus. Michael is in a room down the corridor. Mike Mills, who I never see, is in another.

I am sitting on an uncomfortable chair by an awkward-looking vase of fresh flowers, watching the minute hand of a clock inch closer to our allotted interview slot. Pop stars usually run late. Today – typically, given my nerves – he's running on time.

I only have twenty minutes with him. Twenty minutes is nothing for an interviewer. I'm wondering what anyone can get out of anyone in twenty minutes after introductions, hesitations, and anecdotes going off-piste – it's worse still when you want to get something organic, natural, conversational going. I know that the interview length is probably there because Michael is understandably bored senseless with the ritual, having been asked the same questions endlessly over three decades. And that's before he'll notice his interviewer flush-faced, knackered, gawping, terrified of messing things up.

The previous night at a pop quiz, a friend and former colleague, Andrew Harrison, had given me a brilliant idea about how to approach Michael. 'Give him an exit interview, as if he did a normal job. As if he was leaving it at last. As if he can't wait to get out the door from those blokes he's had to sit alongside for ever.' I had gone home, and scoured the internet past midnight, finding plenty of shiny, corporate examples. I would ask Michael what improvements he would make to the workplace, how he'd found his workmates. Could his bosses have done anything differently? I could veer off-topic at times, but the format would keep the breezy humour levels high.

Last night, it had felt perfect. But now, with one minute to go, I am trying to forget an interview Michael did a fortnight ago. This was with journalist Pete Paphides for the *Guardian*. Pete Paphides is lovely. Pete Paphides wears cardigans. He is one of the kindest, most sensitive, least aggressive music writers in Britain. He was unlucky. The first question he asked was which band member broached the idea of the split. '[Michael's] piercing blue eyes deaden,' Pete wrote in his piece, instantly introducing the reader to the mood of the room.

Things got worse. Michael responded to a question about the huge pressures of fame after *Out of Time*. Pete quipped that it could have felt like being in an iron lung. Michael snapped back: 'I could apply that [metaphor] to public transportation if you want to take it further. It gets you where you want to go but it might not be the happiest ride. Or sweaters. They keep you from catching colds. Come on, really, that's a little harsh.' It's never good being told 'come on' by someone you're interviewing. 'I wouldn't compare my thirty-one-year career with my best friends to dialysis,' he added.

I'm sitting in a posh hotel corridor, about to spend twenty minutes with the man whose voice, lyrics and songs I obsessed about most through my adolescence. I'm about to throw a comic question-and-answer format at the feet held by all those hands at the Sepulveda Dam.

I don't want to go into the hotel room on my own, and see him at the end of the bed. I want to grab my bag, get up, twist on my Doc Martens, head home –

'All ready.'

Michael's publicist nods at me from the door. I walk over. Michael Stipe stands up from a sofa and adjusts his black-framed glasses. He is wearing a grey striped shirt, neatly buttoned to the neck. I walk towards him, stretch out my hand, let his fingers take mine.

*

Thankfully, I survived. He was in a jubilant mood. He loved the format. He took the piss out of his pretension. He only stopped at one point. 'Hey, I'm really sorry to do this . . . but where did you get that T-shirt?' Mission accomplished.

At a few points, he opened up. I dropped in some little details about the making of R.E.M.'s 1985 album *Fables of the Reconstruction*, when they were being produced by Joe Boyd in a miserable studio in North London's Wood Green, and he told me about the terror of being a gay man back then; how he'd heard about the threat of men being put in internment camps back home in America; how every time he got a cold he thought that was it. Even when I was making him plumb his worst moments, he was disarmingly lovely. Maybe he'd decided to be friendly because it was his last day in the gig, but I didn't care. And yes, this fan asked for a selfie.

When I think now of the young man I used to pine over in the 'Drive' video, I wonder how the adulation of fans like me really affected him. What does the recognition of that love do to a person? Does it mess with your mind? How do you cope with seeing people clock you, watching their jaws drop, knowing you have helped to mould the emotional shape of their lives? At that point, I didn't know that Michael would keep coming back to promote R.E.M.'s album reissue campaign, keep returning to a spotlight that he had willingly left. He's also done more interviews since, about his photography and art. It's as if he wants to keep communicating after all. I still want to ask those questions about the relationships with his fans. One day I hope to.

*

That moment should be the beautiful ending to this story. The grown-up fan has met her beloved, found him wonderful, made him smile, closed a chapter, moved on.

In December 2017, I was invited to a twenty-fifth anniversary playback of *Automatic for the People*, now remastered in Dolby Atmos surround sound, in the basement of a Soho film studio. I was there with Nadia, a dear friend I had met not on a fan forum, but the vast, terrifying hive of human activity that is Twitter. We bonded through our shared love of pop music, of *Smash Hits* and the Pet Shop Boys, but most of all, our love of R.E.M. Michael Stipe and Mike Mills were in the room. We weren't quite Lucy Bennett and her friends backstage in Europe, but the proximity to the men together felt surreal. Nadia and I kept looking at each other and stretching our mouths in comedy grins, still fourteen in our giddy little hearts.

Before the playback, Michael talked about how presenting himself as a vulnerable man, while fronting one of the world's biggest rock bands, was a very new concept when *Automatic for the People* came out. He added that his mum was in the audience today. There was a Q&A afterwards. I nervously held up my hand, asked what his mum's favourite song was. She even answered: a song about water emptying to the tide, life passing before our eyes, 'Find the River'.

In the bar afterwards, R.E.M.'s publicist pushed me

in front of Michael. I hadn't wanted that to happen. She then told him who I was, that we'd spoken before — and he said hi, was polite, but, unsurprisingly, given the many journalists he'd met, he didn't have a clue who I was. Then he turned to Nadia, touched her scarf over her red duffel coat, and told her approvingly, 'That's working.' She offered a nonchalant thanks while screaming inside. She remains far cooler than me.

Twenty-five years earlier, I'd have been upset not to have been remembered, but at that moment in the Soho studio, it didn't matter. We'd just spent fifty minutes listening to *Automatic for the People* in incredible detail, the songs surging around us like a series of giant, cleansing waves. Twenty seconds into 'Drive', I was, embarrassingly, in tears. It felt like I was being submerged in an ocean from the past — their past, my past, our pasts, all together — but I was also spotting new features in the mix, in basslines, guitars, drum patterns, harmonies, melodies, tiny textures, rustles, breaths. I didn't want to see Michael Stipe in the room: I wanted to see Michael Stipe in my head. I wanted to feel him making connections between my brain and my body, experience those old journeys of dopamine and oxytocin rushing through.

This was a world I knew so intimately, but now I was experiencing it in high-definition. I was like a face in the 'Drive' video being given full colour, being tied to the racks eagerly, happy for my inner world to tell me where to go.

Track 6

Radio-Activity – Kraftwerk

How Music Moves Us Together

One night in June 1997, when I'd not long turned nineteen, I was a tiny speck in a gargantuan, dark tent, held tight within swells of people and a tide of cyclical, rising electronic sounds. Never before had I experienced music this loud. Sounds seemed to be shuddering each and every synapse inside me, electrifying every cell.

Our new masters were high above us, in suits gridded with green neon lines, directing us to their precise, metronomic rhythms. I hadn't taken any drugs. I didn't need to take any drugs. I'd used the last dregs of my student loan to get a place on a coach to a field outside Luton. I knew it was one of my greatest ever decisions. That pulse, that room, that sound: I was more exhilarated and energised than I had ever been in my life.

*

The song that took me to that field was something I'd first heard two years earlier in my family's front room, a net curtain away from where I last saw my dad, a floor below where I'd daydreamed about Michael Stipe, a hall away from where I'd seen Adam Ant and Neneh Cherry on TV. I heard it downstairs because this song wasn't my discovery to keep to myself; it was Chris Vanstone's, my friend who lived a mile away in the lower half of the village. Every Friday, Chris would walk up the hill past the Reverend James, the post office, my grandparents' house and the old phone box, carrying four cans of Foster's in his rucksack, piles of CDs rattling away on the top. He'd knock on the door, charm my mother, cross the terrazzo tiles, come in, pass me a can and sink into the corner of the sofa. We'd sit in the dim light by the curtains together, crack our ring-pulls like old gits, take turns to press play.

I liked *The Mix* before Chris had even got it out of its case. He'd bought it second-hand in Llanelli Market, a place more known for rugby ephemera and pork pies than pop music discoveries. A figure loomed from its cover, shot from below, with a humanoid head and torso and spindly robotic arms. Its typeface – which said KRAFTWERK and THE MIX – was already outdated, made out of blocky pixels. It reminded me of the Spectrum 48K computer Dad bought when I was small. Dad and I had played games on it together, and made simple tunes by using the bleep command, enabled by pressing shift on its satisfying, rubbery keys. You added two numbers after each note, one for its pitch and one for its length. Every now and then after Dad died, I'd try to do this on my own, make tiny memories sing from its speakers.

The Mix was released in 1991, almost a decade after my father had bought that computer. Technology had moved on. This artwork hadn't. Later I would come to realise Kraftwerk probably knew from day one that they were creating their own nostalgia, revisiting the recent past to reflect on their identity.

Still, *The Mix* recalibrated eleven old Kraftwerk tracks to bring their sounds more in line with contemporary techno and club culture. It began with a new version of 'The Robots', originally released in May 1978, a few weeks after I was born. In this new version, a sequence of tones buzzed and whirred, ending with a pitch gliding upwards, sounding like a computer booting up. Next came 'Computer Love', a song predicting online dating that had a melancholy sheen; then the playful 'Pocket Calculator' and its Japanese cousin, 'Dentaku', before the beatific ride that was the nine-minute edit of 'Autobahn', a few easy junctions in warm weather, stripped down from the more startling and frightening twenty-two-minute album original.

Then there was 'Radio-Activity'. 'Cher-no-byl,' purred a vocoder-enabled vocal. 'Har-ris-burg. Sell-a-field. Hi-ro-shi-ma.' I knew three of those names from my terror of nuclear war as a child, from dancing to 'Two Tribes', from hearing about *When the Wind Blows* and a terrifying film called *Threads* that no one was allowed to watch any more, so I heard in the schoolyard, because it'd make us all want to end it all. I wouldn't discover that Harrisburg, Pennsylvania, was the site of the Three Mile Island accident in 1979 until years later, when the internet was at my disposal. 'Discovered by Marie Curie,' the voice added, in a higher, clearer tone. 'It's in the air for you and me.'

I loved the beat more than anything, how it hammered away at my head and twitched away at my muscles. It was chillingly high-pitched and urgent, and it made me desperate to move. Uh-oh, I realised: this was dance music. In my teens, I'd learned to avoid dance music. Dance music was for girls who wanted to beat me up in the playground. Girls who most of the boys in school fancied. These girls now wore fluffy bras and hotpants in Escape, the glossy super-club in town. I barely got my legs out at home. Snootily, I dismissed them.

By then, I was going to a big tertiary college five minutes' walk from my house, making friends with students from a huge area around Swansea, Llanelli, the Gower and the Welsh Valleys. Our canteen felt like an anthropology experiment: likeminded souls congregating in different corners, wearing the colours of their tribes, leaders assigning themselves, hoping others would follow. I'll never forget the day one of the peacocks in our gang strutted in, yesterday's long, grungy curls replaced by a short, shaggy Damon Albarn crop, and the collective gobs-open shock at the pop culture paradigm shift.

Ringer T-shirts, coloured trainers and sixties-to-seventies charity shop chic were becoming our armour. Blur, Pulp, Elastica, Oasis, Supergrass and Sleeper were our messy-haired guides. We searched for them in *Select*, the *NME* and the *Melody Maker* on the canteen's Formica-topped tables. Their words were our gospel. Many of these artists had a cheekiness and a confidence about them, which we wanted to absorb by osmosis – virtues that would soon turn, for some, into fame-addled egomania.

I was pretending that dance music hadn't bled into my life at that point. I was deliberately forgetting how much I'd loved side 4 of *Now That's What I Call Music 11* in early 1988, an anthology's recognition of the arrival of house music, packed with acts like The Beatmasters, Cookie Crew, Krush and Jack 'N' Chill. I had drawn rave culture smileys on my pencil case, adding the word 'acieeeed' with lots of Es, in tribute to how much I loved D-Mob and Gary Haisman, without realising what acid was. In my R.E.M. years, the odd dance track would sneak through into my acceptable pile – Robin S's 'Show Me Love', the Prodigy's 'No Good' – but I knew these songs weren't really mine, and that they should be resisted. I'd picked my kinfolk. I was alternative. Indie. Non-mainstream. I brushed off the knowledge that many indie acts I loved were already in the Top 20, or signed to independents part-owned by majors.

Persistently, dance acts started to break down my steely resolve. Here came Underworld and Orbital, the Chemical Brothers and Leftfield, making tracks that were mind-twisting, innovative, undeniable. Their penetration was partly thanks to *Select* championing dance music constantly, whatever the Britpop-dictated revisionist histories say. Then there was the faceless democracy of the radio, our collective gateway to other voices, who we relied on so much when our friends weren't around to chat to. Friends often weren't around in the evenings in those years before we'd passed our driving tests and before mobile communications existed, when the landline phone was deemed too expensive to use for more than twenty minutes by our mams and dads – the cord spiralling under the door when we were allowed, our information superhighway to paradise.

On weeknights, Steve Lamacq and Jo Whiley, Mark Radcliffe and Marc Riley, Andrew Collins and Stuart Maconie became our constant companions. On Fridays, John Peel would pop along too, like a wayward and wilful but lovable grandfather. Some DJs were at the mercy of playlists, programmers and station controllers, but that period in the mid-nineties was one of huge change for Radio 1, when freedom in the schedules started sneaking in. It's also where I heard Underworld's 'Born Slippy', Orbital's 'The Box' and Leftfield's 'Open Up' for the first time – and of course, I taped them.

Taping the radio was everything to me when music wasn't easy to find. The cassettes I made in the mid-nineties were peculiar jigsaws of old songs and new, their sequencing at the mercy of the order in which I'd heard them, and the whims of my tastes. Most of my friends made these tapes. We'd talk in the canteen every morning about the night before, referring to the DJs as if they were our confidantes, although we were in awe of them too. They gave us presents – aural miniatures of delight – without us asking. The process of receiving them felt miraculous because it felt accidental. We'd caught that song at that precise moment because of serendipity – we could have easily been off having tea, or being bollocked by our parents for leaving our bedrooms in a tip, but we weren't. I remember first hearing Kristin Hersh's 'Your Ghost' in this way, having sat down on my bed seconds earlier, my fingers rushing to press the record and play buttons together – and then Michael Stipe's harmonies appearing in the chorus, and me convinced I was going to faint. I didn't hear that song on the radio again, nor find it in the shops, for weeks. But I heard it repeatedly after that thanks to a precious thin sliver of sepia tape, encased in white plastic.

Of course, I had heard ABBA and Wham! in this mysterious way as a child. I heard many more groups that I loved when I had my own radio and cassette player in my room, when I turned its dial all by myself.

*

Soon after radio broadcasting to the public began, academics tried to analyse the effects of hearing voices across the airwaves. Hadley Cantril of Columbia University and Gordon

W. Allport of Harvard published one of the first books about it, *The Psychology of Radio*, in 1935. Radio was a tool for human expression, they wrote, that people had craved: 'If radio had not somehow satisfied human wants, it would never have attained its present popularity, for it is only the interests, the desires, and the attitudes of the listeners that can vitalise the vast inhuman network of the air.'

They also suggested that radio, more than any other medium of communication, was capable of forming a 'crowd mind among individuals who are physically separated from one another'. In times of social disruption, 'the radio voice of someone in authority, speaking to millions of citizens as "my friends", tends to decrease their sense of insecurity'. This could create a mob mentality in the listeners, they warned, or 'congregate clusters of people sharing and giving expression to a common emotion'.

In April 2021, I read a special issue of *The Wire* magazine, which was all about the future potential of radio. It explored how digital stations and home broadcasting had exploded the possibilities for specialist programming – but it maintained that the relationship between broadcaster and listener remained all-important. Radio producer Alannah Chance nailed this perfectly to the journalist Jennifer Lucy Allan, calling radio, beautifully, 'a bodily kind of medium'. She went on: 'The best presenters sound like they're talking to you . . . and yet [they're] always aware that it's an audience. It's this continual interplay between intimacy and reality.' In other words, the music radio presenter is speaking not just to one individual 'you', but to many 'yous', tying people together in different places, countries and circumstances, almost by magic.

Around the time my radio obsession was at full height, I found Kraftwerk's *Radio-Activity* album on cassette in my local record library in Llanelli. (I loved record libraries. I remember going to the one in Swansea as a small child, in the orange-and-cream Victorian grandeur of Alexandra Road, the wide stone steps that Dad must have struggled with, the heavy smell of the PVC protective vinyl sleeves.) I remember being intrigued by *Radio-Activity*'s cover: an old image of a black-and-white machine, rendered in white scratchy lines. It made me think of the picture of pulsars on the cover of Joy Division's *Unknown Pleasures*, another recent, adored find, and I still wonder if Bernard Sumner, or Peter Saville, Factory Records' designer, thought of *Radio-Activity* unconsciously when they made it.

The cover image turned out to be of a radio speaker, with two button dials sitting either side of the album title. I put the tape on and thought that maybe it was damaged – there seemed to be silence. But here came a slow, deep pulse, very gradually speeding up, then suddenly, it was fast, settling into a regular rhythm. The first track was called 'Geiger Counter'. A Geiger counter was for measuring levels of radiation. A Geiger counter always projected audible clicks because radiation is always present in our lives – in the sunshine, in the soil, even in people. But if the clicks were accelerating, as they were on this album, then there was something else going on.

Behind this beat came a crackle of noise, like radio inter-ference, then the unhurried rise of a drone of synthesised voices. The drone was sublime, both heavenly and fright-ening, as if a sequence of numb, wordless screams had been stretched out to the scale of a sinister, un-angelic choir. A wetter, lighter beat replaced the low pulse, then a new, high tone flickered in, like a ticker desperately trying to record, process and convey information. I found out years later that it was the title being spelt out in Morse code. 'Tune into the melody,' the clearer voice said to me then, at seventeen, as the title track emerged in its original form, a very different beast to the 1991 remix.

I looked at the album cover again, and realised that its title had a double-meaning. 'It's in the air for you and me' was a lyric as much about communication as it was about annihilation.

On the cover of the original issue of *Radio-Activity* from 1975 – the edition I found in Llanelli library – was a radio first brought to market in 1933. Its name was the Volksempfänger: the People's Receiver. An electronics engineer from Munich, Otto Griessing, had made it at the request of a new government minister, Josef Goebbels, who had set up a department for public enlightenment. Six years later, Griessing received 10,000 Reichsmarks for his invention, dressed in the uniform of the Nazi's paramilitary *Sturm-abteilung* wing.

By 1942, 16 million Germans owned a Volksempfänger, through which they heard regular bulletins from Hitler, as well as German music he endorsed, like Wagner and Beethoven symphonies. Three years later, the Nazi project had collapsed, but the radio infrastructure they had relied on was still in place. In 2018, the composer and sound artist Robert Worby made a brilliant BBC Radio 3 documentary about what happened next called *Radio Controlled*, which showed how radio was rehabilitated as a new tool, used for creativity, not control.

One of Worby's interviewees was writer Alex Badenoch, author of *Voices in the Ruins: West German Radio Across the 1945 Divide*. He summarised the situation the country faced after the war: 'It's hard to imagine, but on top of this shattered country, there was a layer of sound . . . the new Germany was coming [over] on the airwaves before it was actually on the ground.'

Worby then summarised radio's potential very simply: 'Because the past had been so terrible, people in West Germany turned to the future.' But first he looked back to what the future was going to be before the Third Reich came along, exploring the radiophonic and electronic compositions that had bubbled up from German avant-garde culture in the twenties. When post-war radio stations turned to new sounds to distance themselves from the Nazis, they rehabilitated these older experiments to carve out new directions. In Cologne, a West German radio station, the Westdeutsche Rundfunk, built the first ever electronic music studio. Here, a studio technician, Heinz Schütz, created a piece using magnetic tape and faders, to prove the worth of the project. It was called '*Morgenröte*', which translates as 'The Red of Dawn', signifying the start of a new day. Its sounds and its title had echoes in a track Kraftwerk released in 1974, '*Morgenspaziergang*' ('Morning Walk'), where electronic buzzes and flutters swirl around a re-creation of birdsong and a blissful, simple flute melody, shaping a sense of optimism from new beginnings.

Kraftwerk were born into this disassembled but creative post-war world. Ralf Hütter was born in August 1946, just outside Düsseldorf, less than a year after VE Day. His bandmate Florian Schneider was born the following April, moving to Düsseldorf from south-west Germany when he was three. Both had wealthy, artistic parents – a textiles trader for Ralf, a renowned architect for Florian – and in an interview with Karl Dallas for *Melody Maker* in 1975, around the release of *Radio-Activity*, Ralf described where they grew up. '[It was] In a sort of crossroads between France and Germany, so we were exposed to the *musique* of Paris as well as the electronic music of Cologne. That is what opened up our ears in the late Fifties.'

Kraftwerk wanted to make the idea of adventurousness in sound accessible to all. 'A lot of art music excludes itself from the audience,' said Florian, in the same interview. 'We had to devise a kind of music it was possible to play onstage. We like simplicity. The simpler the better.'

'We like to be understood also,' added Ralf, a wish I found moving when I first read it, and still do.

This simplicity extended to the everyday, contemporary subjects Kraftwerk focused on in their songs: the autobahn, the computer, the man-machine, the radio wave. Their lyrics and sounds were nuanced and probing, exploring the positive and negative potential that could simultaneously simmer in all of these things, in unpretentious, stark language. This wide-eyed curiosity has kept me captivated by Kraftwerk for all these years. They are always making your brain whirr as you feel yourself want to dance.

They also sang often in their mother tongue, German, to try to create an identity away from the Americanisation shaping West Germany. Never did they deny the horrors of their national past. 'We certainly represent the generation with no fathers,' Ralf told the *NME*'s Chris Bohn in 1981. 'We have nobody to listen to, no old wise men or anything.

We have to impose every question on ourselves and try to find the correct answer.'

In the same interview, they also mentioned how they enjoyed stripping their songs back to basic elements, tunes and beats. 'Our music is very primitive – the German word is *geradeaus* (straight ahead) and that is the best word for it,' Ralf said. 'Simple means a little stupid, minimalistic means reduced, but *geradeaus* means, you know where you are going, and you try to get there as fast as possible.'

The beat was certainly fast – and it travelled as it was being understood and translated. By 1981, Kraftwerk's music was well-known in US cities like Detroit, thanks to the support of popular DJs like Charles Johnson, also known as the Electrifying Mojo. The young Juan Atkins would listen to this radio show in his bedroom. A year later, he adopted the term 'techno' to describe the music he made with his friend Richard Davis, under the name Cybotron. Their 1983 track 'Clear', a whoosh of slippery, silvery moods, sampled Kraftwerk tracks 'The Hall of Mirrors' and 'Home Computer'; this followed Afrika Bambaataa and the Soulsonic Force's 'Planet Rock' a year earlier, which twisted together 'Numbers' and 'Trans-Europe Express' into a twitchy party floor-filler.

Thirty-five years later, I read Matthew Collin's history of global dance music, *Rave On*, in which he writes about Juan Atkins, and his friends Kevin Saunderson and Derrick May, aka techno's holy trinity, the Belleville Three. Their music was 'attempt[ing] to dream another potential destiny into existence' from their impoverished home town, Collin wrote. He'd been there in the eighties, and 'nothing could really prepare you for seeing the ruins of Detroit up close, unless perhaps you grew up in post-war Bosnia and Herzegovina'. Or perhaps, if you were Ralf or Florian, in the RAF-ravaged cities of post-war West Germany.

Collin also wrote about the Berlin Love Parade, a festival that began the summer before the Berlin Wall fell, reclaiming a liberal spirit on the streets where Hitler had once held his rallies. Berlin is still a global centre of techno today, played in uncompromising clubs like Berghain and operating far away from social media and corporate culture, where music is allowed to create secret sonic wonderlands.

Electronic music has also captured new audiences in recent years within tumultuous political systems in places such as Iran and South Africa, Collin explained. He asked South African DJ Jake Lipman if electronic music can change things. 'It allows people to express themselves in a positive way. How can it not be good?' Lipman said. 'He responded so vigorously that he almost knocked our coffee cups off the table,' Collin added.

And behind all this geopolitical energy was the beat: its radical pull, its potential to create new perspectives. The beat on the 1991 version of 'Radio-Activity' was trying to deliver its message with revolutionary speed, eight months after the reunification of Germany, with Europe as a unifying force, while still in the shadow of the existence of the atomic bomb. As techno entered the mainstream in the nineties, it stretched out to different audiences, its messages limber and lean.

I still feel as drawn to the beat of 'Radio-Activity' now as I did in 1997, when Chris and I took a coach with my university friends to the Tribal Gathering Festival in Luton Hoo. We arrived at Kraftwerk's tent two hours early, as Two Lone Swordsmen entered the intense final leg of their eight-hour sound-system set – a fitting preparation. I lined up with other geeks in anoraks, waiting for the raving crowds to descend, and I felt terrified when the people came pouring in. But then we danced together, triumphantly, at the greatest gig of my life.

We were a mix of ordinary Joes, glammed-up ravers, trance hedonists and Detroit techno royalty (the techno tent next door closed for the duration of Kraftwerk's set so Jeff Mills and Kevin Saunderson could watch their heroes). As the machines pounded, fluttered and palpitated, it felt like we were all pressing, jamming, slotting together. We were in Kraftwerk's world, their tracks built from everyday pieces of ours: they spoke of business, numbers, money, people, pro-grammed machines, borderless travel, a universal language of shared references against swathes of thrilling rhythms.

But they also recognised that modern life was infused by fear, and the threat of things we could not control. That night, they played 'Radio-Activity'. Before it, a low, fuzzing electronic voice told us that Sellafield would release the same amount of radioactivity as Chernobyl every five-and-a-half years. Then the beat came again, rocketing us away from the dread, giving us a reminder of the revolutionary potential of music to help us communicate with other people. I found myself in those sentiments, in those rhythms, as the track took over.

*

I first heard Dr Sophie Scott, Professor of Neuroscience at University College London, on a Mixcloud post of a talk from the Ambient Salon, a regular event, hosted by music journalist Joe Muggs at London's Standard Hotel. In that talk, Scott spoke of hearing as our 'social sense', and how vibrations from the movements of so many parts of our bodies, down to the inner architecture of our ears, aligned motion with music. She also talked about how humans have voluntary control of many aspects of their bodies, and that responding to rhythm could be a by-product of enacting that control.

Rhythm seemed to be something highly specific to humans, she said – other creatures mirror some behaviour, like yawning or laughing, but they can't mirror each other like humans do when we dance. I drop her a message online to probe further and we speak on the phone early one afternoon. 'There does seem to be debate about a handful of other animals that show responses to rhythm, but that's very, very rare. But if you watch people walking together, they will follow the steps of each other, so you actually align yourself with people around you, even if you don't mean to.'

Dancing is what is known in psychology as a 'joint action', Scott says: an act in which multiple people coordinate their actions in space and time to perform a task together. 'There's something about joint action that's really important for humans. It's not neutral: it's positively enjoyed and increases your sense of affiliation and affection with that person.' In his 1995 book, *Keeping Together in Time: Dance and Drill in Human History*, historian William McNeill coined the term 'muscular bonding' to demonstrate this connection; such bonding has been considered very powerful in human societies for centuries, Scott adds, but it's mainly discussed, as it is in McNeill's book, around demonstrations of authority. Army drills are well-documented as making people feel part of a unit, for example, even though they're rarely done anywhere else than on the parade ground. But adding a musical soundtrack to *any* display of movement increases our capacity to bond. 'Music is important in our social lives, essentially, because we're social primates, and humans have endorphin-based social bonding – and when we have the opportunity to dance with other people, that can become a virtuous feedback loop. Dancing isn't just about moving your feet either. It's a whole-body enterprise.'

A few months later, I come across the work of James Kilner, another neuroscientist at UCL, who attends music festivals like Latitude and Bluedot in what he calls his Lab In A Van, and give him a call. In these settings, he does simple science experiments on individuals, and he's always surprised at the numbers of people who come along, 'willing to find out how their bodies work'. His dream project would be to scan everyone's brains while they are dancing together. Test conditions do not usually fit in with rave settings, he adds – somewhat mournfully – plus the equipment and an assessment of variables and control groups would be difficult. Still, he would love to see whether people's brains function in synchrony in these environments, as he expects they do.

'The way the majority of neuroscience experiments are conducted involves the subject being very isolated,' he says, requiring individual fMRI scanners or assessments, which is a source of frustration for him. 'Whether the same effects would be observed in social situations than what we see in private tests . . . well, my suspicion is, we wouldn't see most of them.' Like Scott, he says that human beings are very social, and that this is a rare quality in most mammalian species. 'And you know, why is that? What makes us tick along? And I keep coming back to the fact that there's no human culture that doesn't have some form of music and dance, so it does indicate that music and dance must be relatively fundamental to who we are.'

I tell him that 'Radio-Activity' made me feel ten feet tall as I danced to it that night at Tribal Gathering. After Kraftwerk, I did something most unusual for me too: I stayed up all night. Next came Orbital, then Daft Punk: both sets were incredible, full-body experiences. At 8.30 the next morning, I was found in the jungle tent dancing on my own to Fabio and Grooverider when we were meant to be getting our coach home. Many people in my party had been fuelled by cheap pills, Ecstasy or speed; they were already asleep in their seats. My fuel had been two beers, two coffees and an egg bap I'd had at 5 a.m., from a caravan lit like a Hopper painting against a sky of deep dawn blue.

I love thinking back to this night because my relationship to dancing before then had often been fraught. Discos in primary school, upstairs in our local rugby club, a cavern of burgundy velveteen, were often excruciating; me wearing a sleeveless polo neck and a gold necklace, desperately wanting to fit in, my arms and legs feeling awkward, unwieldy. I only felt happy when we all held hands in the middle-eight of Dexys Midnight Runners' 'Come On Eileen' and ran the circle inwards and outwards. I'd still feel happy dancing to that now. It was our adolescent Hokey-Cokey.

I felt similarly pained at discos at our comprehensive school theatre, when the DJ played Right Said Fred's 'I'm Too Sexy' and the *Grease* Megamix; we were expected to do grisly sex-pumping mimes along to the music. Dancing was often cast as part of a ritual, I realise now, as a way of playing out heteronormative gender games. I liked dancing when it was in an environment where I felt supported or comfortable, not sexualised. I was more interested in jumping around to the Happy Mondays' 'Step On', yowling along to Rozalla's 'Everybody's Free', looking like a wally, my hands scooping the air.

Things got better in tertiary college when I met Dan Cuthill, a boy from up the road in Penllergaer, who became one of my dearest friends. He expanded my musical horizons more than any person and, twenty-five years later, his Spotify playlists are still introducing me to new treasures. At sixteen, he made me copies of albums by strange women like PJ Harvey, Björk and Tori Amos, and told me about Barons, the indie club in Swansea on Thursdays, and The Indie Thing, on Saturdays, opposite the train station. Dan's mother was a local nurse, also called Jude, a woman my mam knew and loved, as did everyone else. So I was trusted to stay over at Dan's house, where I could enact my rebellions on solid, safe ground.

What transpired in those early mornings after nights out in town was innocence drizzled with bottles of Hooch, freezer pizzas and 3 a.m. viewing sessions of *The Beat* with Gary Crowley. Big Jude – as she came to be known, for reasons of conversational ease – would wander in in her dressing gown, squish in between us with a mug of hot tea. We would be lying dishevelled on the sofas – hair awry, eyeliner smudged – as the videos rolled past our eyes, because the night that had preceded such flopping had been all about the dancing.

When I hear the Breeders' 'Cannonball' now, I'm back on the first floor in Barons, just below the over-35s night, known locally, and terrifyingly to me now, as Grab a Granny. I can see the long bar to the left, the black walls, the piles of coats at the sides of the room and in random heaps on the carpet, the pleather booths on the far side where I hoped to drag boys I fancied, and, miracle upon miracles, occasionally did. If 'Cannonball' came on, Dan and I would bounce out of wherever we were – from a booth, someone's arms or someone's mouth, carried along by the taste of lager-tops and Silk Cuts and the smell of CK One – to the dancefloor, acting out the song's twisted turns and tics, loping to its louche grooves. Kim Deal's languid bassline held the chaos together, letting us slouch together in time, sharing its language of sound with good friends and strangers. Some strangers had the same haircuts as us, and some didn't: Swansea back then was a haven for goths, and some of the grunge fans wouldn't let the ghost of Kurt Cobain go. Our limbs were happy to mirror theirs, though. The beats kept us together. They opened up our ears and our eyes to each other.

*

At my happiest, dancing always takes me out of myself. In Barbara Ehrenreich's 2007 book *Dancing in the Streets: A History of Collective Joy*, she discussed the work of nineteenth-century anthropologists, terrified of the trance-like state dance could invoke in non-Western cultures. 'A place beyond the human self . . . or what was worse, a place within the human self,' she wrote, waspishly. She also discussed the idea of 'collective effervescence', one of the foundations of Émile Durkheim's 1912 treatise *The Elementary Forms of Religious Life*, a book which instituted him as a founding father of sociology. Collective effervescence remains a useful concept when we're thinking about the levels of joy that can come with dancing. To me, 'the ritually induced passion or ecstasy that cements social bonds' is a good way of pinning down its effects, although I don't think that collective effervescence necessarily forms 'the ultimate basis of religion' as Durkheim believed. Many people I know would very willingly worship in a black room under strobe lights nevertheless.

Reading Durkheim today, I'm reminded of the moments of total abandon I felt at my first festival, Glastonbury in 1995, with Dan, his younger sister, Helen, and a minivan of other ringer-T-shirt-clad friends. Big Jude was driving us – she had always wanted to go. She'd look after us, she told our mams, and so she did.

Off we went. Dan and I had just turned seventeen, and it was a glorious weekend: perfect sunshine, a slight breeze, our tent parked right by Michael Eavis's farm above the Pyramid Stage, a mam back at base if you needed anything, watching the main stage from her camping chair. We had a secure foundation for total freedom. We watched PJ Harvey strut onto stage in her neon-pink cat suit, cyan-eyed, hollering 'Meet Za Monsta', before playing one of the most staggering sets I've ever seen in my life. Gaz Coombes' sideburns anointed me with sweat in Supergrass's front row, as their punky pop songs, the little rascals, turned me into a soggy hot mess. I watched Elastica's Justine Frischmann – my style icon, with the short haircut I craved, hanging over her dark eyes with the right combination of sharpness and loucheness – thrashing her guitar right in front of me as day turned to night.

On the Saturday night, I also watched a band headline who weren't meant to be there, for whom I had gig tickets in Cardiff University Students' Union a few months later, singing a new song about the normal world feeling very, very, very far away. 'Sorted for E's and Wizz' was about feeling disconnected in a rave, but I felt absolutely rooted to my core, to the essence of the moment, for the length of Pulp's set that night, in my homemade shift dress, Doc Martens and tortoiseshell glasses. The promised headliners, The Stone Roses, couldn't play because their guitarist, John Squire, had fallen off his mountain bike and broken his collarbone. We joked that Candida Doyle, Pulp's surly keyboard player, had pushed him off. Instead, we were hearing songs about weirdos like us, making a move, making it now, coming out of the sidelines, hoping this was the way all our futures would feel.

*

That was the first of many festivals for me. Ten years later, I returned to Glastonbury with Dan, just the two of us, where another headliner had to pull out on Saturday night. Basement Jaxx replaced Kylie Minogue, who had just had a breast cancer diagnosis. Big Jude had died three years earlier. We felt her absence keenly in those huge Somerset fields. I remember how closely Dan and I clung to that year's crowds, to the shared reference points of lyrics and melody we had with total strangers as we sang along to the Futureheads, The Coral and Interpol. We let music and our movement with other people remind us of the gifts that Big Jude had given us.

Minogue finally played Glastonbury in 2019. I watched her set at home in Wales, Dan watched it from his flat in London, and we texted throughout. When Nick Cave came on to sing 'Where the Wild Roses Grow' with her – a song Dan and I had both loved in our tertiary college years, now sung onstage by two friends who had passed their half-centuries – I cried like a baby. On the screen we watched people dancing who were the same age as we were in that distant, glorious summer, as well as people our age, the age Big Jude was when she took us to Glastonbury, and older. In their faces was a joy we understood, even though we were sitting in front of our televisions in our distant living rooms. Songs ripe for dancing were vessels for our shared histories, for all people who grew up around pop culture. Live music brought our feelings for these moments of connection into the energetic present, and the sharing of music by listening to it, watching it, moving to it, fostered a supercharged sense of community.

Watching Kraftwerk at nineteen, in an initially unsettling, unfamiliar environment, performed a similar function in a more dramatic way. Their name in German translates as 'power station', which I adore – because that night, they truly gave me, and so many other people around me, electricity. They made me realise that music – physically, psychologically, spiritually – can galvanise us collectively, help us fit in. Music eased my transition into adulthood after that, encouraging me to expand my horizons and experience new kinds of music as the century and millennium came to a close.

That Kraftwerk gig encouraged me to go and see Mogwai and Atari Teenage Riot's aural assaults. Their electronic momentum pushed me towards Steve Reich's juddering minimalism, and the softer, sinister textures of Low and Stars of the Lid. They also helped me venture out into the wider world when I moved to London to study for a Masters' degree at twenty-one, to find so much pleasure at clubs like Trash, where The Stooges' 'I Wanna Be Your Dog' and New Order's 'Blue Monday', euphoric, wayward bedfellows, were played every week without fail, London's trendiest kids screaming on the dancefloor around untrendy me.

Better still, I knew I could enjoy this new music, but not peel away from stuff that I had loved before. I still adored going to indie nights like How Does It Feel To Be Loved? and Track And Field, where I would meet the group of friends that would sustain me through adult life, as well as the man I would marry. Music took me from a bedroom alone to a front room with a friend to dark clubs full of my peers to sunny fields and tents filled with different faces. It gave me joyful foundations to take my life forward, to expand its possibilities, to feel them all pulse in the world.

End of Side 1

The unfamiliar tape was in a shoebox, next to others I recognised – their spines were covered in my teenage, more ornate, purple-inked handwriting. I was back home from young adult life in the big city – walking across the terrazzo tiles through the front porch to the living room into the new extension at the back where my mam, in her efficient mam way, had been doing what we all dread mams doing. She had been 'sorting stuff out'.

Jon had returned from university. Room had to be made for James's things, now that he was a teenager. We lived in a world where people were burning music onto devices that they could pop in their pocket, ripping them from dusty CDs; cassettes now appeared prehistoric. But in the box, there was one without a label, so I took it upstairs, brushing whorls of dust off my tape player, popping it into the long-forgotten deck.

Here were Kim Wilde's 'Kids in America', Roxy Music's 'Jealous Guy', Landscape's 'Einstein A-Go-Go'. The clunk of record and play buttons being pressed together between every song hit my heart like a hammer.

Mam now had slow internet in the house – I looked the songs up – all were in the charts of March 1981. I was nearly three then. Dad was thirty.

Here was something he had made. Here was a story of his life. He had archived those songs in a physical object. I knew I was lucky to have it. It felt especially precious appearing early in this new century when music consumption was changing. I was aware that our experiences were starting to disappear into virtual clouds as songs became much more accessible and available online, as their ubiquity became something we took for granted.

After I found that tape, I wrote for the first time about my father, and our connection through music, for the *Guardian*. It felt like I was letting something play out that I had long tried to silence. Recording that story – writing it down, transferring the power of that moment to a screen and to paper – helped me understand him as a fellow adult. It also helped me understand myself.

It made me realise, too, that we all need tangible things to remind us of moments in our lives, treasured things to reflect on and return to. As adulthood bedded in, I appreciated that songs themselves could function in a similar, beautiful way. Here they still are, waiting for us. In them, here I am.

Track 7

Heat Wave – Martha Reeves and the Vandellas

How Music Shapes Love

In my first years trying to live as an adult in a big city, I listened a lot to a young woman who had just been dragged out of a party in midwinter.

This woman was twenty-one, a secretary by day in a converted old white clapboard house, running the phones, organising the desk diary, sorting out the payroll. At night, she liked to get up onstage and perform in local clubs – that was her true calling, enjoying the sound of her voice soaring – trying to get the feeling she got in church when she was singing and praising the gospel.

But not that night. That night, there was a party going on a few doors down from work on West Grand Boulevard – she was out and it was late, and the spirit of the season was high. But then her bosses came along and begged her, please, Martha – come on, Martha – come back to the office and sing for us in the basement. 'I didn't want to go to work. I was at a party!' she said in an interview for St Louis newspaper the *Riverfront Times*, forty-seven years after that night, which I read when I was well into adulthood, and well-versed in the subjects about which she used to sing.

'But I followed them back over to the studio,' she said. There, she sang about things that felt far from the cold: burning flames, heads taken over by hot hazes, high blood pressure, involuntary tears. She sang about love setting off so many physical responses and extreme reactions. 'It reminded me of the holy spirit,' Martha Reeves said of how she felt singing 'Heat Wave' for the first time in Studio A, in Motown's converted HQ, Hitsville USA.

Since I became obsessed with that 1963 single in my early twenties, Reeves' vocal has crystallised something undeniable to me about the way love's supposed to be. It's an energy that's crackled inside so many people, and at so many different life stages. It's an energy that still creeps up on me when I don't expect it, that still ignites these older bones.

I know love. I have felt it. I still feel it. But is it only something you feel? Or is it something you construct? Or is it both? And can music help it along?

One afternoon in the quiet, book-lined oasis of the British Library, I turned to an eighty-two-year-old American professor for help. This was sociologist Thomas J. Scheff, a man awarded his PhD in 1960, the same year that Motown Records got its name. All his life he had long been fascinated with how people were drawn towards music as a repository of emotion.

In 2011, he published *What's Love Got to Do with It?: Emotions and Relationships in Popular Songs*. 'In [many] years of teaching college students, I couldn't help but notice that for many of them, popular songs held a special meaning, as they did to me when I was their age . . . [they] were more meaningful to them than most of the other arenas of their lives.' Love songs held a particular power, he noticed, so he surveyed this in more detail, undertaking a comprehensive study of love song lyrics over six decades, then interviewing students about what love lyrics meant to them.

Scheff notes how many of the pop lyrics young people clung to evoked unresolved, extreme feelings, which weren't readily or easily discussed in Western societies: about obsessions, fixations, unrequited infatuation. 'Popular love lyrics present a picture of an imagined social-emotional world, and modern societies tend to ignore this world. Since modern societies are highly individualistic, the nature of relationships usually takes a backseat. Modern societies focus on the self-reliant individual.'

Spontaneous emotions entering this environment are generally discouraged, Scheff continues, diagnosed as episodes of emotional liability or emotional incontinence. But in love songs, these emotions are expressed for you, articulated with passion. Feelings of discombobulation and sickness don't sound frightening when they're captured in music. They arrive like the substance of life: when Peggy Lee sings of her fever as a double bass slinks in support, when Bruce Springsteen wakes up with the sheets soaking wet and a freight train running in the middle of his head, when nothing can take away Prince, The Family or Sinead O'Connor's blues.

The artistic value of the individual love songs we like isn't even particularly important, Scheff says. The fact that popular songs simply arouse emotion, 'however mechanically, is probably the main reason they are so excruciatingly important for so many people'. They are useful. They give us places to put our compulsions, our needs, those feelings that hold your body like a vice as you think about someone you want, and feel yourself succumb to psychological paralysis.

Throughout the book, I was struck by Scheff's analysis that love songs were often not about mutual experiences, but being stuck in your own head, and I realise, of course – this is how we experience love, however close we get to another person. We can never get into the heads of the people we adore, but only try to understand them, to share an intensity of connection with them. This reminded me of a book I read at university, the kind of slim volume you'd stick out of your blazer pocket to try and seduce someone raffish and clever, because it was French, and therefore sexy: Roland Barthes' *A Lover's Discourse: Fragments*. Full of breathy exhalations about love and sex, it covers topics like festivity, languor, ravishment and reverberation. It lays out its stall, and its perspective, in the preface. The lover's discourse is one of 'extreme solitude', Barthes writes, in which a person is 'speaking within himself, amorously, confronting the other (the loved object), who does not speak'. Into this private realm, the love song enters like a mirror, showing you that what you are experiencing is recognised, that it is made of dense substance.

When a singer is suddenly articulating words we could not or dare not express, on our behalf, we respond by listening and buying – and of course, Scheff admits, the market responds too. The record industry often turns its attentions towards young people going through these feelings for the first time, a movement that escalated in the fifties as money started to fill their well-pressed post-war pockets. More dramatic expressions of love could also be seen as more comprehensible for the youth consumer anyway, Scheff asserts, especially as calm, reasoned mutuality is an idea not readily promoted by Western societies. 'Even by adults,' he adds, with a withering flourish.

But while we all have intensely individual experiences of the surprises and sensations of love, the idea that other people have felt these feelings, and have had the bravery to express them through songs which are meant to be heard by others, that are meant to be understood, is an incredibly powerful one. Love songs offer the suggestion that we can explore our internal dramas together and accept love's extremes as part of who we are, in collective, celebratory moments. 'Our everyday existence can morph into a kind of work of art,' writes US music historian Ted Gioia in *Love Songs: A Hidden History*, another book I picked up that day in the British Library. 'Music plays a key role in this process, not just as a soundtrack in the background, but as a constitutive ingredient in generational identity and the individual's sense of self. The love song doesn't disappear in this highly charged context – if anything it takes on new power.'

*

I am thinking of a young man trying to find out how he will make his way in the world. His mother and father are entrepreneurs with print, plastering and carpentry businesses in a bustling North American city. His grandfather, a landowner who moved from the South to escape the threat of lynching, was the child of Esther Johnson, a plantation worker from Georgia, and James Gordy, the white plantation owner who enslaved her. James Gordy had another son – not born to Esther but to his legal wife, Mary Ida. Also named James, his grandson was President Jimmy Carter.

In 1955, Berry Gordy, the young man trying to make his way in the world, works in the Ford car plant in Detroit. He's twenty-four, with two failed careers behind him, and he's miserable.

Nelson George writes about the failures shaping Berry at this time in his 2003 book *Where Did Our Love Go: The Rise and Fall of the Motown Sound*. Berry had tried to be a boxer, with limited success. Then he ran a jazz record shop, paid for by all his personal savings and US Army discharge monies, topped up with a loan from his father. It closed after two years.

Disillusioned and bereft, Berry moved on to a job on the factory floor, fitting panels of chrome and beautiful upholstery to cars. To pass the time, he sang to himself, making up lyrics, and realised these songs were becoming earworms. He then found out he could get songs transcribed as sheet music for twenty-five dollars a go (twenty-five dollars today is £180 – not an insubstantial investment).

Two years later, Berry co-wrote a song with his sister Gwen and a friend, Billy Lewis, for Jackie, a man he used to box with. That song was 'Reet Petite'. It became an international hit, getting to number 6 in the UK, and from that single onwards, Berry kept trying to hone and polish singles until they gleamed like Lincoln Continentals. In 1959, he set up his own record and publishing company on a highway in Detroit, in a former photography studio which he bought and converted. He put a sign on the front that said Hitsville USA, making careful adjustments to the body of the building, adding new features, turning it into a perfect star vehicle.

It had taken Berry a while to find his feet with Motown, the label that got its definitive name a year later, and it would take a few years more for it to find its greatest grooves. But success isn't just about the people in the middle of it all, who are spotlit and amplified. It's also about the many other people who play small, vital parts in the story, who contribute to their early, glorious beginnings, that set a rhythm for the later big hits.

*

Love began for me, if I listen to the music in my gut, with Metallica's 'Enter Sandman'. 'Enter Sandman' kept coming to my front door to chat on weekday evenings after school, magnetised to the terrazzo tiles in the porch, always too shy to come in. One night, he brought along a cassette in a bible-black case, holding it tight in his hand. Later that night, I said my prayers, tucked myself in, pressed play. James Hetfield hollered and moaned, taking my hand, trying to lead me to never-never land.

Was what I felt back then love? It probably wasn't. I never knew if it was reciprocated either. It didn't matter. I felt different. My body had a whirlwind of butterflies inside. I liked elements of how that felt – it was like enchantment – but there was something else folded in. There was an empty space in me that needed healing. A soft edge of dread. Fear.

The sensations were there because I knew that this reaction was out of my control. I couldn't turn this boy on and off: he wasn't a whisper in my ear or a face on a screen. He had a presence in my mundane, bodily life. He could suddenly appear in the school corridors when I wasn't prepared for it. He had responses and reactions that could be affected by my actions, or worse still, barely affected at all. What I felt replaying Metallica's *Metallica* that night, focusing on its first track, was something brand new: the recognition of feeling being ignited by a real, tangible human being.

When you start to feel love, 'every song in the universe is addressed to you personally,' writes psychologist Anouchka Grose in her book *No More Silly Love Songs: A Realist's Guide to Romance*. Think of every mixtape you've received from someone you really fancy, or every song you've sought solace in after a break-up, and all the meanings you try to mine from them. Grose writes that songs act differently from messages that have come directly from the object of your affections: we tear our hair out trying to decode every phrase in a text or an email, and show them to friends to help us understand what they meant. Meaning-making becomes important when the meanings behind love seem so hard to pin down. '[And] songs and stories are good because they help to give form to your overwhelming feelings.'

In my experiences of falling in love – sometimes an electrifying, sickening thud, sometimes swimming in balmy waters up to my clammy neck – songs have always felt like solid, fixed things. Their structure and timbre remain the same, we tell ourselves, as when they were originally recorded, and we find comfort in that. But love songs can change, and we can mould ourselves along with them.

When we fall in love, even if it may not be for ever, we find ourselves bending the significance of individual moments within songs to our own specific situations. Taken to extremes, one of the first unnerving signs of insanity is 'that the world is sending you messages', Grose says, but if you're sane, you're compensating for the madness of the world by putting the messages there.

Music without lyrics can also gain meaning in Grose's assessment: its rises and falls can be interpreted how you like. As someone who plays musical instruments still, although not as well as I used to, I also think about the musicians playing those songs, and how we as listeners get lost in the efforts of their labours. These people have committed hours, days, weeks, months and years to perfecting their playing, to make music magical and meaningful for themselves and for others. Some musicians' relationships with their instruments are practically love songs in themselves. They all combine in the transmission of a huge exchange of emotions.

*

I am thinking of a young boy in Edisto Island off the coast of South Carolina. He gets up every morning to sneak into school – a small, two-room building – with his friends. On cold mornings, they light a fire, and play the school piano together. After school, they play in an empty summer house, which has another piano and a dusty double bass, which James Jamerson gravitates towards.

In the next two decades, James will provide the agile back-bone to some of the world's greatest love songs, including the Supremes' sweetly desperate 'You Keep Me Hanging On' and the Four Tops' urgent, longing 'Bernadette'. Then there is the song for which he wrote a bassline on a midwinter night, working together with baritone saxophonist Andrew Terry, a bassline that strutted out of Hitsville USA and down West Grand Boulevard before it took flight out across the oceans.

James Jamerson is my favourite of the Funk Brothers, the shifting collective of seasoned jazz club players recruited by Berry Gordy to be his whip-smart house band. On a recent long drive, I played a two-hour playlist of Motown songs, and I was frequently agog at the slippery slink of James's style. Plucked with one finger, his other hand frisk-ing around the frets, it was full of playful personality, but somehow still strangely effortless, often blending into the background to provide a foundational funk in the service of his fellow players. 'The most important point my father told me: when I'm playing, if I don't feel it, don't play it,' said his son, James Jamerson Jr, in the 2002 film *Standing in the Shadows of Motown*, which told the Funk Brothers' long-sidelined story. 'You know, put something in it. He felt that life was music.'

The film brought to life other characters long forgotten from pop history. They included Richard 'Pistol' Allen, who once burst into a jazz club in pyjamas, dressing gown and slippers, so strong was his desire to play, his sledgehammer four-to-the-floor drums inventing the framework that became Northern Soul's skeleton. There was Joe Hunter, whose piano-playing was full of bright rhythms, as if sparks were flying from his fingers on the piano keys; and the glassy, meshing guitar lines of Eddie Willis, who recovered from polio as a child to play, exquisitely, on 'You Can't Hurry Love'.

When I think of Motown, I also think of Robert White, who composed the famous guitar melody at the beginning of The Temptations' 'My Girl'. Years later he heard it in a cafe while struggling to get work, knowing that something he invented had become part of the landscape, but nobody knew who he was. I think too of Jack Ashford's glistening tambourine in so many Motown songs, each snap of the silver discs setting off shooting stars. I think about the people that play crucial roles in great songs but get forgotten, and the people who play crucial roles in our approaches to love who get forgotten, too.

We're told the love we hope to ultimately find often comes after many false starts, different takes, happy accidents. We all live in that process and play along with it, which means that none of us are ever really singing our love songs on our own.

*

My first boyfriend was Blur's 'For Tomorrow' – a twentieth-century boy with his hands on the rails. Or rather that was the way that I painted him after our four months together had finished. That song had been one of his favourites, and it gave him a mystical sheen after he'd dumped me and quickly started snogging someone else. It made our time together telling jokes, eating chips in the canteen and drinking cheap pints in indie clubs much more mythological. Back then, I was sixteen, my school uniform and fixed braces long gone, determined to create a new version of myself, Jude not little Judith. So, when that first boy had gone, I attached him to a song. It gave my hurt a weight that I could hang on to for dear life, as Damon Albarn sang, in those unsteady teenage years.

Then there was Orbital's 'The Moebius', who I also sometimes think of as Gorky's Zygotic Mynci's 'Patio Song'. Every lunchtime, as he smoked fags by the skips or let off an air-raid siren in the canteen, I was doing extra revision classes trying to get ready for my Oxbridge entrance exams. We pretended we weren't seeing each other, because it couldn't happen because we were so different (oh, to be full of the arrogance of youth, believing that other people would care). He made me tapes of weird Welsh psychedelia and techno and gave me an Orbital T-shirt that I still wear sometimes as part of my pyjamas (its label is peeling, but its colour's still vivid). We're still friends. His wife's great.

My kid likes his kids. He will laugh when he reads this. We're a twist in the fabric of space when time becomes a loop.

Then come the many other songs tied to people who still have a presence in my life, even if that presence is virtual or distant. These songs are linked to people who would still mean something to me if we bumped into each other in the street, taking in the older faces, the grey hairs, the wear and tear of life. When I think of these songs, I often can't see myself in them, nor the men; instead I see stage-sets from the past, abandoned locations for short, intense films. I'm nowhere in Strangelove's 'Time for the Rest of Your Life', for example, but a full glass of Southern Comfort certainly is, at two in the morning, in a student room with wood panelling that extends to the ceiling. In Blueboy's 'The Joy of Living', there's the view from the bus down Oxford's Iffley Road in the winter sunshine. In Looper's 'On the Flipside', there's the statue of Robert Stephenson at Euston station, his hand on the hip of his frockcoat, waiting for a boy to get off a train from the North.

When I hear The Cure's 'Pictures of You', things change. I'm on a motorway on a dark, rainy night, and I can see two people in the front seat, one of them feeling looked after, comforted at last. The next track that appears after that is Tindersticks' 'My Sister': I see a flat in King's Heath in Birmingham, dusty net curtains that were once set on fire while he was making us dinner. I maybe remember those details more readily because he was the first person I thought I could have been with for ever, before I broke up with him at Digbeth coach station to the strains of David Essex's 'A Winter's Tale'. 'Fairytale of New York' also drags me back to that time. Eighteen months is a very long time when you're nineteen then twenty.

Other songs in my life have faded in potency. Kenickie's 'Come Out 2Nite' should make me feel something pivotal, something utterly life-changing, but it doesn't: it sounds like teenage abandon articulated by three girls my age, the lead singer literally only a day older than me, and her big brother. I still have the seven-inch single of it on the shelves in my office – it once belonged to a boy with a close-cropped Afro who made me tapes of Urusei Yatsura, got me to read Aldous Huxley, and tried and failed to teach me the drums. Roots Manuva's 'Witness (1 Hope)' feels warmer: in a flat high up in Dalston, watching the Gherkin being built from our messy, scrappy kitchen, a four-hour spag bol forgotten on the hob, a naïve couple trying to work out how to build a home for two people rather than one.

Other songs that made me feel pain retain a sickly power when I hear them, even when they no longer feel trussed to the people who introduced me to them. Godspeed You! Black Emperor's 'The Dead Flag Blues' no longer brings up the person with whom I self-destructed just before my final university exams: now it's a nuclear apocalypse narrative intercut with panoramas of motorways and service stations, played as I travelled around Britain in the solar-eclipse summer of 1999 to get over him. Badly Drawn Boy's 'Once Around the Block' isn't gut-wrenching rejection at a Manchester New Year's Eve gig a year later, but a spry, gentle song tasting slightly of whisky and smelling faintly of mosaic cushions on night buses.

'Love doesn't have an essence that we can uncover. It has, rather, a set of themes that interact differently in different instances,' writes philosopher John Armstrong in his 2002 trawl through culture and history, *The Conditions of Love*. His is an unromantic assessment, but one which makes sense to me, especially when I think about how songs can act as frames within which we capture scenes from the past. Some memories look gorgeous in them, happy and full of depth and texture. Others are muted and abstract, hemmed in by severe lines. But good galleries of images, surely, thrive on variety. And this variety reminds me of all the people who helped shape who I am today, and the songs I hung on to to get me from there to here.

*

I'm thinking of a young man who has been touring for a few years since his teens. He's got a voice that wings in the air, sounding so tender; he's had a minor hit single with a love song called 'Jamie', but the life of a pop singer isn't for him. He gets stage fright, hates the drudgery of the road, and wants to become a writer instead, fitting lyrics to musical sketches for songs composed by his brother Brian and their friend, Lamont Dozier. He also enjoys foraging for ideas from the time he's spent with women. 'I always thought that females were the most interesting subjects [for songs],' Eddie Holland said to Dale Kawashima for the Songwriter Universe website in 2005. 'I got a lot of ideas from what I learned talking to women . . . I'd ask them a lot of questions. They would tell me little secrets that they usually wouldn't tell other men.'

To write, Eddie would lock himself away, close the curtains and enjoy the fact that he didn't have a telephone, like some of his hipper friends. There was, he added in that 2005 interview, a commercial imperative behind his decision to try and win over women with his songs, but there was more to it than that: 'I was also drawn to that sensitivity.' Women later came from all over America to meet him, he claimed – if that actually happened, it can't have hurt. 'They said: "We want to meet you because you understand us."' He also wrote 'Heat Wave', the song Martha Reeves sang in Motown's Studio A, that Berry Gordy knew would be their breakthrough hit, that James Jamerson propelled into the heavens, so I have an inclination to believe him.

When I think of 'Heat Wave' – which is, on most days, my favourite love song of all time – I can't think of a time it's not been in my life. It's so well-known, it almost feels like a part of humanity's collective folk memory. Motown's biggest singles keep travelling into tiny corners of the world through the smallest networks – bar jukeboxes on soap operas, or regional radio stations on dull weekly commutes – into the memory banks of disparate families and friends. The music of 'Heat Wave' has always spoken to me of tentative forward motion, from Andrew Terry's fabulous, squelchy baritone saxophone onwards. He comes up into almost every note from the semitone below it, like a little kid sneakily opening a door when he's meant to be asleep, saying hey, I know I'm being cheeky, but I'm here.

The song pivots from its bouncy opening bars to a first verse which plummets us downwards. Here comes tension in a mournful, minor key, then the 'burning' arrives; 'desire' starts to fill up from inside. The bassline lifts from the fourth note to the fifth to the tonic of the scale, the grounding root – the way a minor key melody usually resolves itself

– but then it crashes back down again to repeat the same phrase, to return to the emotional quicksand. Here is a young woman finding herself stuck in a pattern: she has to pull herself up. Then the bassline rises tone by tone towards the chorus, and the major key appears out of nowhere – and Reeves emerges glorious, elated.

The joy I find in 'Heat Wave' is its cycle of doubt and delight, worry and wonder. In the chorus, Martha sings about not being able to stop crying, but sounds like she's almost relishing that release. I love the contributions of Rosalind Ashford and Annette Beard, the Vandellas, adding their own exclamations behind their friend's proclamations, some of them gutsy, rallying *oohs*, others hand-holding enthusiastic encouragements. 'It's all right, girl!', 'Go ahead, girl!', 'Can't miss it, that's love, girl!' they sing at the end of the song, trying to fight their way through the mix, but I hear them, and feel my shoulders happily relax every time they appear. I'm reminded of the women who stand behind their friends when a feeling is on the cusp of volcanic eruptions, who share their excitement when it's needed, who hold their hands, tenderly, tightly, when it all falls apart.

'Heat Wave' also reminds me of the last time a big relationship in my life was beginning. I was a young girl at a party in midwinter when our love ignited. I'd known him since 2001, and first seen him onstage with a band in London's Betsey Trotwood pub, playing a set before my friend Catrin's group, who were, fittingly enough, called The Loves. I caught two songs at the end of the set. He had a high, intriguing voice, a nice face. He was taken. I went out with a school-friend of his for the next two-and-a-half years, until one day we kissed – and suddenly he was everywhere.

He was everyone. Whenever I was with him, it was love, something surging inside.

*

I am thinking of a woman in an ivory dress trailing to the pavement, her matching shoes already sullied by the dirt outside the pub in Islington's Chapel Market. She is wearing a gold hairband, onto which is stitched a cream silk flower, and has a glass of gin and tonic in her hand, spiked by a silver straw. She passes it to a friend. It is time for the first dance with her husband: their first song.

They stand together on the small dancefloor, look at each other, hold hands, start to laugh at the embarrassment of it all. Cat Power's version of the old doo-wop song 'Sea of Love' starts to play. They have picked it because it was a track on the first mix CD he made for her seven years earlier, wrapped in red paper. It is dreamy and intimate, a song that demands a couple hold each other tight, rest their heads together for comfort. This also helps them ignore the staring eyes of the well-wishers. At two minutes nineteen seconds, it is also mercifully short.

A slightly out-of-tune autoharp accompanies Cat Power asking someone to come with her to the vastness of the water, because she wants to tell them how she feels . . . and then it is done. The song's brevity is one very unromantic reason why it was chosen.

Also, one song cannot sum up a love story. One song which requires you to perform, and for other people to watch you perform – their eyes drooping sentimentally – may not be the way many people want to express how they feel about love. As the woman in that scene, I had talked with the man by my side about the songs for our wedding for hours, days, months, to try and use things that said something about our love, while being aware that these songs would be vibrating around other people. The song I wanted to share with them most was the one that came after 'Sea of Love' on our wedding night, the one that joined us all together on the dancefloor, that two people who loved each other didn't have to perform alone. There are also songs we didn't use because they were too personal, songs that are as much part of him as the way I think of his eyes and his smile and his hand in the small of my back. He emerges from them, all together, loud and bright and true.

He is Jim White's 'The Girl from Brownsville, Texas', his hair curling on the sheepskin collar of his corduroy jacket, his kisses tasting of the strawberry milkshakes from Burger King on the Tottenham ring road. He is 'Seven Days' by Dexys Midnight Runners, which always makes him dance. Love, you don't dance enough. I love it when you dance.

You are 'How Can We Hang on to a Dream' by Kathryn Williams when you were living in your dad's house, while you made us our first curry, her small, beautiful voice accompanying our tentative steps. You are 'Low' by California after things went wrong for a while. You are 'Spiders (Kidsmoke)' by Wilco when we got back together. You are Colleen's 'Summer Water', the sound of everything being renewed, the song I would walk up the aisle to six years in the future.

We are The Zombies' 'This Will Be Our Year', Smog's 'The Well', Duke Ellington and John Coltrane's 'In a Sentimental

Mood', Gene Wilder singing 'Pure Imagination' on the *Willy Wonka* soundtrack, the first film we watched together on a rainy Sunday afternoon, hiding away, feeling like we were children again. Hearing it as we left the register office on the day we got married was one of the best feelings of my life, holding each other's hands, holding our breath, making a wish, counting to three.

'Heat Wave' is ours too, but 'Heat Wave' is also mine, and it is also everyone else's. To share what love feels like, in our hopes and dreams or our memories and our everyday realities, is one of the greatest gifts life can give. So, when our first dance finished that evening in April 2011, and 'Sea of Love' gently ended, and we pulled briefly apart, and I heard Richard Allen's drums burst into life, I knew we had made the right decision. Joe Turner's piano keys started to sparkle and we saw our friends' and families' faces light up – those few seconds igniting something in all their minds that urged a physical response, a leap from a chair, a mad dash from the bar – and I grabbed your hand. I was a girl in midwinter, a boy in an old photography studio, a child in a schoolhouse, a writer listening to women. I was 'Enter Sandman', 'The Moebius', 'Pictures of You', 'Witness (1 Hope)', 'The Girl from Brownsville, Texas', 'Spiders (Kidsmoke)', 'This Will Be Our Year', 'Pure Imagination'. I was a cacophony of dazzling, deafening, incredible sound, a whole life. I was love, feeling it, becoming it, as it burned in my heart.

Track 8

Gilderoy – Shirley and Dolly Collins

How Music Makes (Some) People Write

On a stormy London night, a year into my thirties, I stood in a basement, facing a crowd. My hair still wet from the rain, I stiffened my arms by my sides, lifted my neck in the air, and looked at waving rows of wooden chairs, each occupied by a hardy, solid drinker. Many of them were straight-backed and barrel-bellied like irascible sailors. They held their pints tight in their hands, like harpoons.

By this point, something I had dreamed about since my days of reading *Smash Hits* had been true for six years: I wrote about music for a living. The little girl who had folded a piece of shiny cardboard in half to tell her dad who was number one now had other people reading her words, connecting with her innermost thoughts about songs that she loved. But that evening, I was getting ready to do something very unusual for my job. I was about to sing about a young man being hanged.

The song I was singing was about a young woman who had loved a young man, who wanted the memory of his 'bonny'-ness and his 'rakish'-ness preserved. They had been together as teenagers, but he had done something terrible, and now death must come. It was my job to feel the young woman in the bone of my jaw and the flex of my tongue, to think about a song that had existed in some form for hundreds of years, and deliver it in a way that made it new and meaningful. The next day, I was going to sit at my desk, probably with a hangover, three coffees and two rounds of toast down, to tell the readers of the *Guardian* how I learned to be a folk ballad singer.

My job was full of odd assignments like these, but I also now encountered musicians in real life – I didn't usually have to become one myself. Recently, Robert Plant had made me a cup of tea in Nashville, with his shirt half-undone, checking first whether I wanted my teabags to be PG Tips or Yorkshire, while singing to me a portion of the Welsh hymn 'Myfanwy'. Björk had offered me half of her Pret A Manger fish salad in Manhattan, curling her socked feet like a cat underneath her on a sofa. Cat Power had rolled out of her central London hotel bed as our interview was ending and scampered into the en-suite bathroom, pulled down her knickers, peed loudly, and kept talking.

But that night in the basement of Cecil Sharp House, the London headquarters of the English Folk Dance and Song Society, at their monthly singaround session – where people take it in turns to sing, by heart, unaccompanied – my usual situation had been reversed. Tonight I was swapping places with the people I interviewed, putting myself in the position of what they did for a living, giving myself up to the roar of the crowd and (if I was particularly unlucky) the critics.

I also felt extra responsibility that night because the song I was singing had been chosen for me by a singer I had come to love in recent years. She had first performed folk music in the early fifties, then travelled to America to record music which ignited the folk and blues revivals and the development of rock and roll. She had championed medieval music and dance, and later would give talks about how the working classes, women and marginalised communities should be a big part of folk history. Shirley Collins had recorded 'Gilderoy' in 1978 with her sister, Dolly Collins, for their third album together, *For As Many As Will*, and it was still one of her favourite songs. When I first heard their version, its tone of unaffected simplicity, despite its musical sophistication, felt startling but transcendent.

I was new to folk then, having spent a lot of the early 2000s listening to louder, brasher music like electroclash and post-punk. I loved finding obscure songs in those genres on new compilations, then moved on to acid-folk anthologies like *Gather in the Mushrooms*, with liner notes by Saint Etienne's Bob Stanley, and Honest Jon's *Never the Same*, where I first encountered the earthy might of Lal Waterson. From there, I stole the 2006 reissue of Shirley Collins and Davy Graham's *Folk Roots, New Routes* off my boyfriend, and plundered Shirley's archives further: in 'Gilderoy', her direct, translucent vocals rose up from the song like clear balloons, holding a steely, quiet composure against her sister's piano.

Around the time that she recorded it, Shirley had a traumatic break-up from her second husband, the folk musician Ashley Hutchings, and started suffering from dysphonia, a voice disorder which had a catastrophic effect on her ability to sing. When we spoke about 'Gilderoy' in 2009, she had only recorded one vocal, on a song called 'All the Pretty Horses' for the experimental group Current 93, in the last thirty years.

But folk music wasn't about one voice anyway, she insisted. I remember being in one of my usual, unconventional spots to do phone interviews as we spoke, snatching time between assignments on the Duke of York steps beside the ICA in central London, tucking my legs under my body to avoid tourists, a notepad balanced in my lap, an in-ear lead wired messily into my Dictaphone (this is how freelance life goes). From Shirley, I was learning about traditional music being passed down from less dominant cultures throughout the centuries, and about the fight for songs not to be sanitised, for them to retain their raw messages. Folk music was about the other voices that had sung these songs through those centuries; more than anything, she said, they're the voices you acknowledge in your head when you're singing.

By this, she didn't mean that I should be like a mystic speaking in tongues, but rather a blank canvas, allowing an old story to bleed its way through. 'You have to sing these stories without ego or affectation,' she put it, bluntly. '"Gilderoy" has lasted hundreds of years. All you have to do is trust the ballad itself.'

I'd first met Shirley a year earlier in 2008 in her adopted home town of Lewes, not far from where she grew up in Hastings, for a piece about a weekend festival she was curating at London's Southbank Centre. We'd drunk from stout pots of tea, and she was a lively, wicked and wonderful seventy-four. She'd told me about the folk songs her family would sing to her and her sister when they were tiny, including in an Anderson shelter during the Second World War, and about her song-collecting trip through the southern states of America with renowned folklorist Alan Lomax in 1959, which would produce songs later to become well-known on the soundtrack of the 2000 Coen Brothers film *O Brother, Where Art Thou?* We'd talked about how upset she had been by him not crediting her work properly in his memoir (she had written her own, *America Over the Water*, to counter that, in 2003). 'All he said was, "Shirley Collins was along for the trip." It made me hopping mad . . . I was part of the recording process, I made notes, I drafted contracts, I was involved in every part.'

Shirley's determination to correct misguided narratives impressed me, as did her lack of interest in using these corrections to elevate herself to a higher status. 'Forget the sheen, trust the song' was her mantra about singing, but she also applied it to her life – don't make things about embroidery or embellishment, just try and tell people their stories directly. The quiet profundity of this statement stayed in my head like an earworm over the years; I felt I could apply it to my work as a music journalist, even though I'd also felt compelled to go to extremes in my opinions around the time we'd first spoken. The era of comment culture had begun, and there was a sense that people had to sell their ideas to others more shrilly to stand out in the internet's noise. Access to music and the right to reply had also moved online. Circulations of music magazines were dwindling. Music journalists had to learn to shout louder.

*

My first brush with music writing, years earlier, felt far away from this world. Admittedly, it just involved typing, but typing up something I found wildly exciting. At fifteen, I had a job at my local weekly paper, the *Llanelli Star*, as a Saturday morning editorial assistant. At 11 a.m., I had to embark on a weekly covert operation: to walk the five minutes into town, then head quietly to the counter at the far side of Woolworths, where a girl, slowly chewing gum, would give me a piece of paper, off-white, punched with holes on the side, folded tight. I'd take it back to the office, open it up like a treasure map, offer its contents up to the office hard drive with one chipped-nail-varnished finger. It was the first news of that week's Top 40. It was the summer of 1993, of Gabrielle's 'Dreams', Take That's 'Pray', Madonna's 'Rain'. If only the Woolworths girl had been around when I had to find out what was number one in January 1984.

Still, it took ten years from that point for me to become a music journalist proper; I had many false starts on the way. At eighteen, a lecturer sent me on a one-off music journalism workshop in Swansea, with *Mojo*'s then-editor Mat Snow (Mat said I had promise, but I never contacted him again, nervous about what to say). A year later, I went to the first music reviews meeting of term at my university newspaper (I wrote one review, of Baby Bird's debut album *Ugly Beautiful*, and never went back).

I was scared of not being good enough. Or it was worse than that: I was scared of being *thought of* as not good enough. In my head, music writing had to be about communicating my love of songs, in a network of likeminded souls, and I didn't feel up to the grade. Music writers felt like gods to me, gatekeepers to a magical world beyond a plush velvet rope, and of course so many of those writers were men. People like me – geeks from Swansea who didn't know anybody famous – shouldn't be allowed to wander in.

In 2020, academics Paula Hearsum and Martin James – an old *Mixmag* journalist himself – explored how the god-like cult of the rock critic had emerged in *The Bloomsbury Handbook of Rock Music Research*, in a chapter called 'The Rock Press'. Even from the early days of music magazines like *Metronome* and *Billboard*, which were first published in the late nineteenth century, 'the journalist's role as a cultural intermediary within contemporary commercial systems between the music industries and the music press was transparent,' they explained. In other words, coverage swirled around sheet music production schedules and nascent radio programming back then. Fast forward to 2022, look at the plug for a product at the end of every newspaper and magazine article, and not much has changed. The music business and music writing feed (on) each other.

The *New Musical Express* also started the first singles chart, a Top 12 at first, in 1952; journalists were bringing people's interest in specific records, by Al Martino, Louis Armstrong and Vera Lynn, to public attention. As the music business grew, they also started fighting battles on behalf of the songs that mattered most, and the debate about what constitutes musical authenticity took off. This occupied jazz-dominated titles like *Melody Maker*, which was threatened commercially by the rise of rock and roll. The intertwining of music and politics in America, and then across the world, through the rise of civil rights and the counterculture, also underlined just how serious music could be, and how much it meant to people.

Alongside came the rise of New Journalism, and writers positioning themselves in their stories, layering them with literary devices, becoming stars in their own right. Gay Talese's 1962 *Esquire* cover story, 'Frank Sinatra Has a Cold', became a touchstone for music writing. It famously didn't feature Sinatra himself. What it did include was a lot of intricate detail about the industry machinery supporting Sinatra, and lots of Gay Talese.

By my late teens, I knew the names of all the heroic figures from the 'golden age' of rock writing, who emerged in the post-gonzo journalism era of the seventies – all of them, Julie Burchill aside, were white men. But the first thing I read of Lester Bangs, on a website accessed by my wonky at-home dial-up connection, was about Debbie Harry. 'She may be there all high and mighty on TV, but everybody knows that underneath all that fashion plating she's just a piece of meat like the rest of them,' he said. The second was about my beloved Kraftwerk. It festered with what I assumed Bangs thought was whip-smart xenophobia, wondering if their electronic approach to composition was 'a final solution to the music problem'.

It took more dial-up digging on my part to find out about Vivien Goldman, Caroline Coon, Maureen Cleave, Penny Valentine, Robin Green. Women soared in music journalism history too, but they were often hidden behind the search engine algorithms. But the internet did give me the confidence to join forums, meet likeminded people, and also to email someone whose liner notes I loved: the founder of Shinkansen Records, Matt Haynes, who had put out a compilation in 2000 called *Lights on a Darkening Shore*. I bought this one rainy lunchtime in Virgin on Oxford Street a year after moving to London, loving the picture of Lots Road power station on the cover. I then discovered online how Matt had co-run another independent label, called Sarah, which had released songs I knew and loved from mixtapes made by friends, like 'Pristine Christine' by the Sea Urchins and 'Emma's House' by the Field Mice.

I met Matt at a gig. He was quiet and nervous, but on the page, he almost became someone else – I found the statement he had written when Sarah folded, after a hundred releases dead-on, and loved it. 'It's ours to create and destroy how we want,' the notice railed, in an advert in the *NME* and the *Melody Maker*, 'and we don't do encores.' Matt taught me that writing about music could be transformative, could give me a place to put my feelings, so I asked him – feeling terrified – if he wanted to make a fanzine with me. It would be about London, the city which was giving me so much music at that point, in the basement of the Neal's Yard Rough Trade, the many shops of Portobello, and the racks of Sounds of the Universe. We called it *Smoke: A London Peculiar*. In issue 1, I wrote about how Handel and Jimi Hendrix had lived side by side in the same street in Mayfair (separated by two centuries), and sent a copy to the offices of a new magazine that had me as excited as *Smash Hits*: a monthly called *Word*, who featured us in its pages a month later.

As a reader from issue 1, I had felt like part of *Word*'s welcoming club: it was like *Smash Hits* for older, geekier grown-ups, reinforcing that the best music writing, to my mind, always creates a community. It makes us excited about new details, research and fresh perspectives, and makes us want to share this new information thoughtfully with others, while it challenges us too. It's happy to dismantle hoary myths rather than recycle them, and above all it is entertaining, making us smile, laugh, gasp, sigh, well up, punch the air. It doesn't encourage us to stand apart from others, straight-faced and smug. It makes us want to enjoy this glorious stuff all together.

That summer, *Word*'s reviews editor, Paul Du Noyer, asked me for a drink, and told me he wanted me to freelance for

him. A few months later, a miracle: I was offered a job helping him in the office two days a week, squeezed in between
postbags of CDs, piles of back issues, and rotating office
thrones on which music journalism royalty sat, talked and
cackled. They were the very best of men. Editor Mark Ellen
was all bright eyes, twitchy limbs and itchy enthusiasm.
The business-savvy David Hepworth enjoyed playing the
dour, sour Yorkshireman, until he let his cap slip and his
soft-as-soap kindness slide through. And Andrew Harrison
– Andrew Harrison! – who had edited *Select* magazine –
Select magazine! – the bible of my tertiary college years,
was in the corner, tapping away at his laptop ferociously at
160-beats-per-minute, peering over his glasses like a techno
Joe 90. Paul was my mentor, though, a suave, silver-haired
Scouser who had joined the *NME* after replying to their
much-mythologised punk-era advert asking for 'hip young
gunslingers'. He was quiet, thoughtful, funny, a world away
from Nick Kent and Lester Bangs. He is still my favourite
writer, not as known as he should be, and the one I most
look up to.

In my first year at *Word*, he gave me Paul Simon and
Brian Eno's back catalogues to review, because he wanted to
read an opinion not from the 'same old bloke again who had
known this stuff all his life'. He kindly crossed out my many
adverbs, and taught me about the powers of observation, as
well as the mining of facts. His Amy Winehouse interview
in 2003, published in the month I started at the magazine,
tells us more about the woman she was then, and would
become, than the many caricaturing character assassinations
that followed (it's archived on his website online). '*Frank*
was her diary of a torrid adolescence – she was just nineteen

when it was recorded – sung with the funky melisma of a jazz veteran and the glottal stops of a mouthy schoolgirl on the Piccadilly Line,' he wrote. I loved this sentence too, saying so much in a few words: '[*Frank*] is a story-teller's album, in the way that great country & western records used to be.'

Years before I spoke to Shirley Collins, Paul had made me realise what the best kind of music journalism should be. It shouldn't be about sheen. It should be about properly listening to the songs and using your words to help get them heard.

*

I fell in love with music writing, and as the next few years raced along, I started to write for newspapers too, but the landscape for the medium was changing. In 2006, the *Guardian* launched a new online platform, Comment Is Free. Writers were encouraged to pitch opinion pieces that would attract comments, and in June 2007, I rattled one out for them arguing that Jeff Buckley was overrated. I read it now as by someone trying to fit into this new atmosphere of provocation and reaction. He was the 'Christina Aguilera of alternative rock', I raved. He was a 'hit-and-miss songwriter'. He'd purposely created a myth around his early days playing guitars in small venues, or rather, 'sold a merry story about him being a male Phoebe out of *Friends*, falling out of coffee shops and dive bars'.

I still think Buckley, although talented, is overrated. I also love reading pieces that deconstruct a band's mystique, like J. R. Moores' fantastic dissection of Idles for The Quietus, which made me think of them very differently. I have written angry, critical pieces, of which I am proud, including one on the use of domestic violence as a marketing tool for Rihanna's 2012 album *The Unapologetic*, published in *The Stool Pigeon* and The Quietus compendium *Grace Under Pressure*.

But in 2007, I was a twenty-nine-year-old wanting to stand out a bit more, and I regret the hook of the piece – the topical reason for its publication – put across with blunt force by a staffer in the sub-heading. 'I used to love the singer with the dextrous voice and the twinkle in his eye,' it still reads, like the beginning of a dodgy novel. 'Ten years after his death, I've realised the truth.'

I didn't think about the piece's longevity online. I didn't realise that words could go into the top hits of a search engine and hang around there for ever. The Buckley critique has been the piece I have had the most emails and tweets about over the years, all of them written in raging, aggressive language. Every single one of them has come from a man. 'What the fuck have you done with your life to be so incredibly disrespectful to a wonderful musician?' started one email about it in 2020, thirteen summers after I had written it. The sender hadn't considered the time that had passed. 'Either quit being a journalist or find a new fucking job. People like you make me sick to my fucking stomach. I wish nothing good for you.'

Online, old blogs loom like headstones, our words carved hard and fast, resisting the forgetful fog of our memories. That said, I have had worse reactions. In 2009, a few months before the singaround, another man wrote a long blogpost criticising one of my pieces, saying that he wanted to kick me so hard that my uterus would rupture. My crime was to use the word 'twee', which had been included in a headline accompanying my piece, a gentle, short article about an indiepop tribute album to Bruce Springsteen.

By this point, everyone in my generation was on Facebook. Twitter was taking flight. Smartphones were lighting up. The days of complaints being sent into the *NME* and *Melody Maker* by letter, to be ignored or ripped apart by an editor, were long gone. Suddenly everyone could write about music, tag the writer as they were doing it, use their words as weapons if they wished.

This is partly why criticism has lost its teeth. In the late 2000s, the idea of the journalist as a gatekeeper to new music and information about musicians was being finally, comprehensively dismantled. Fans were gaining more agency as they could access music more easily; then musicians started writing on social media directly, without being reined in by their managers or agents. Tracey Thorn made a point I'd never considered before when I interviewed her onstage in 2019. 'We were all scared of you,' she said. 'For years, it was up to you how to show other people who we were.'

I've trodden more carefully with my interviewees since then, trying to think about what lives on in the printed word, while not shrinking away from asking tough questions. (I've not always got it right either, but I keep trying.) Paul taught me to listen properly, read your notes back, and be honest about your reactions when you're considering what the interviewee said. Shirley also made me think about ignoring any sheen that arises from your status as a published writer, any nip of narcissism that sparkles inside you. You should also see past the sheen that emanates from the fame of your subject. You have to be true to the story of who you are speaking to, however complicated it is, but still be respectful.

This meant that of course I was going to ask Richard Thompson about his ex-wife and former musical partner Linda, and why he hadn't detailed their famously hellish tour together from 1982 in his memoir, *Beeswing* – but also that I would do so without sneer or snark. Clearly, I was going to ask Noel Gallagher why he loved Paul Weller so much, but wasn't inspired by him to be more adventurous with his music – most people preferred to bathe in his banter – but try to do it kindly. I was going to ask Peaches about how a cancer diagnosis in her twenties made her reassess her life, and skyrocket her filthy, fabulous art-pop (she was one of the kindest interviewees I've ever met, sorting me out a hotel when my flight home was cancelled, treating me to drinks in some of Berlin's tiniest, messiest bars). And obviously, I was going to ask Elton John about how much he hated the Tories after his post that suggested that on Instagram, even though I'd been told he probably wouldn't want to discuss that again. 'I'm 74 years of age and I just don't get this unfairness and this ridiculous ability to lie through your teeth every fucking minute of the day,' he ranted about the government in reply.

And of course I was going to ask Chrissie Hynde why, as she wrote in her autobiography, she took 'full responsibility' for her gang-rape by a group of Hells Angels, during an interview in which we also discussed her revived love of painting. We didn't agree, but the conversation was cordial, respectful, a proper dialogue. She painted a portrait of me at the end of our time together in her studio and sent a print of it to me later by post. 'Crude, but honest!' she said of it, by text. It felt like a description of her character, and our encounter.

In our brave new digital world, fans can read the words of their idols directly, wallow in them, treat them like gospel; they can then speed messages back, and if they are lucky, get a like or a response – or as behavioural neuroscientists would see it, a reward. And this is where things, as always on the internet, get tricky: our communication about music online is driven by the craving of approval. This applies to all of us, me included, hoping that our voices are heard, liked, shared and responded to. Perhaps this is why so many reviews now feel more positive than they were in the past, why critics get nervous about being scrupulous about the flaws, faults and failures of artists they love.

A case in point: in late 2021, I was asked to review ABBA's first album in forty years, *Voyage*. I was so excited – but then I listened to the album and was deeply disappointed. I gave it two stars. It was a hard review to write, on account of my fandom – I also knew it'd probably get higher ratings elsewhere. I was right. Tweets told me I hadn't listened to it enough, that I wanted to spoil people's fun, that I didn't understand the power of joy. I replied with links to gushing essays I'd written about the merits of 'Dancing Queen'.

I thought about how Sean Parker, the founder of Napster and early player in Facebook's success, once talked about how social media companies warped our connections with others. He explained that their algorithms often used 'a social-validation feedback loop, exactly the kind of thing that a hacker like myself would come up with, because you're exploiting a vulnerability in human psychology'. It was no longer as acceptable to disagree, even on something as subjective as a set of songs. Likes and other reactions introduced later, Parker said, gave users 'a little dopamine hit', strengthened their sense of being on one side or another.

The idea of the online dopamine hit made me think of Catherine Loveday again, telling me how dopamine also flows in greater quantities in situations relating to love, sex and obsession, as well as in our relationship with music. Perhaps this is why fans have felt so passionate, and so extreme in their opinions, about musicians online in the last fifteen years. It's as if a little criticism of their beloved becomes huge in the heightened glare of the screen, as if they're getting annihilated for ever.

*

In 1763, Thomas Percy, a grocer's son from Shifnal in Shropshire, was the first to write in print about Gilderoy – a rogueish man hung high for his crimes, despite being adored by many people. He did this in *Reliques of Ancient Poetry*, a collection of folk ballads and popular songs that captured the public imagination, later influencing the poetry of Samuel Coleridge, William Wordsworth and Sir Walter Scott. Some of the ballads were taken from a folio put together a century earlier, he writes in its preface, which he had found on the floor of the house of his friend, Humphrey Pitt: 'This very curious old manuscript, in its present mutilated state, but unbound and sadly torn, &c., I rescued from destruction . . . I saw it lying dirty on the floor, under a Bureau in ye Parlour: being used by the maids to light the fire.'

I wonder if the folio's origin story was embellished. This is always the risk, as I've learned, when we try and tell our tales: we have to keep our stories under control. The folio has survived the centuries nevertheless, and is stored in the Rare Books section of the British Library, its individual pages carefully mounted and covered in gauze.

Percy attempts to describe who Gilderoy was in his introductory notes to the ballad, although variations in storytelling in different parts of the country make this a hard task. '[He was] a famous robber, who lived about the middle of the last century, if we may credit the histories and story-books of highwaymen, which relate many improbable feats of him, as his robbing of Cardinal Richelieu, Oliver Cromwell, &c.,' he begins. In one account, Gilderoy shoots Cromwell's horse, breaking his leg, and gives Cromwell his life back after sending him home on a donkey. In another, he is hanged until dead on a gibbet much higher than his peers, because of the severity of his crimes. In yet another, he cuts the throat of his mother, because she won't give him money, before raping his sister and their servant.

These are 'no more than the records of Grub-street', Percy rants, referencing the area around London's Old Street which boomed with tabloid-style periodicals in the mid-eighteenth century. Different publications magnified and twisted his reputation, as they still would today.

If we trust songs, Percy says, 'Gilderoy' was more likely to have come from sixteenth-century Scotland. A ballad about him exists in a 1733 Scottish songbook, the *Orpheus Caledonius* – a lost title for a great metal album, for sure – which includes a verse mentioning Mary Queen of Scots being alive. She died in 1587. This ballad has similarities with the version Shirley Collins sang over 250 years later, in that it details his beautiful garters, that Gilderoy and the female protagonist were born in 'one town together', and how he was her 'heart's delight'. The violence is absent, but other action is present, including some 'indecent luxuriances that required the pruning-hook'.

One suspects, as Shirley Collins did when she first read about 'Gilderoy' in a 1909 folk society journal, that Percy is suggesting the removal of sex from the song. The version Shirley came across had six lines missing from the third verse, substituted by asterisks, she writes in her 2018 memoir, *All in the Downs*. 'Obviously it was considered too frank for the delicate, albeit hypocritical sensibilities of Edwardian England.'

Shirley has always been at ease with sexuality in folk-song. Her version of 'Hares on the Mountain', the first song of hers I loved, from *Folk Roots, New Routes*, has an eroticism that is gentle yet insistent. 'If all you young men were fish in the water/ How many young girls would undress and dive after?' she sings, each word delivered like lightning hitting a still pond.

The version of 'Gilderoy' that she sings is one she found herself in the library of Cecil Sharp House in the seventies. It was transcribed by Lucy Broadwood, a woman from a wealthy musical family of piano manufacturers, and collected from Henry Burstow, a Sussex shoemaker, bellringer and radical thinker who had a prodigious memory for songs. It has a verse about Gilderoy taking the female narrator to a field, putting his hand around her 'waist so small . . . and down we went together'. When 'he had done all men can do', the song continues, 'he raised and kissed his joy'. When Shirley sings it, you feel a woman's desire, her sexuality, coming through, the words emerging with vitality after so many years of suppression.

Broadwood had been an important figure in the English Folk Dance and Song Society's early years, her collecting preceding Cecil Sharp's efforts; she was even its president in the last year of her life, before her death in 1929. Her files were in a terrible state, though, Collins recalls: 'to my horror and anger . . . [they were] locked away in a little side room . . . loose sheets of paper scattered on the floor, covered in dust and with every sign of being nibbled by mice'. Shirley had fought to be in the library in the first place, as working-class people – especially women – weren't exactly encouraged to join. In the mess of the room, Shirley also found a letter that Henry Burstow had later sent to Lucy, full of tenderness and modesty; it too had been nibbled by mice. Collins admits in her memoir that she stole it, only returning it a few years ago, knowing it finally would be safe.

In 2009, Shirley told me that 'Gilderoy' had always meant a lot to her for another reason: for the weight of its feeling. 'I love this girl's devotion. I also love the line, "What a pity it is a man should hang." It's quite a shallow phrase on the surface, but when you look at what happens next – his beloved saying she will go to his grave with a sword by her side – you realise the depths of her pity.' As I learned to sing 'Gilderoy', I realised it was a vehicle for powerful feelings that women are not allowed to express as readily as men, including lust, rage and strength. I also felt it was a song which spoke of the forgotten work of Lucy Broadwood, and of a difficult time in Collins's life, in which she was delivering a narrative which spoke volumes to her.

As I sang it that stormy night in the basement, in my own, unfiltered, Welsh-accented way, I remembered how it felt to be seventeen, with a hand around my waist so small. I remembered rogueish boys that mams and dads loved – it had to be 'mams' in my story – and how I felt about them, and there, facing the crowd, I still felt like me. In my nervousness, I made a few mistakes, but the sailors weren't irascible at all; in fact, they urged me on. We all sang the last two lines together.

In recent years, when I've written about music, I've tried to do so more candidly, more directly, than I used to. I've relied more on facts than opinions to help a story come to life, finding dustier corners in my research – in old interviews in print, film or on the radio – that deserve a scrub-up. I love making people seem more three-dimensional. They're usually more interesting that way.

These days, music makes me want to write about people whose stories deserve deeper exploration. When I interviewed Marianne Faithfull in Paris, I made sure to emphasise the details of her brilliant, lesser-known albums as much as her glorious, sweary, taking-no-prisoners personality. I already knew everything there was to know about her and Mick Jagger, as did everyone else, and I knew that the mentions of those clichés lessened her. I only mentioned her response to an early pregnancy's effects – she had spent years trying not to speak about the Stones, she said – and a photo of Jagger in the toilet, after Marianne pointed it out. 'Best place for it!' she hammed.

Another interview that meant a lot to me was with Teenage Fanclub in 2016. I'd been moved by how much their fans rallied around the three singer-guitarists, Norman

Blake, Gerry Love and Raymond McGinley, and I wanted
to explore where that tender loyalty came from, as well
as little details that amplified the band's very ordinary
beginnings. Some of them I still remember fondly today:
a New York lawyer for Geffen Records calling Raymond in
the council flat he still lived in with his mum and dad in
1991, expecting him to fax him back straightaway, assuming
he was suitably wealthy and connected; Raymond didn't
have anywhere near the money to buy one. Then there
were Gerry's early memories: of the family piano being
taken away by the council, and what it was like to grow
up near the huge, smoking Ravenscraig steel plant in
Motherwell — which featured in the video to the band's
Top 20 single 'Ain't That Enough', a year after it was closed.
The plant then stood as a memorial on the cover of their
2003 greatest hits, the first album I ever wrote about for
Word magazine.

They were a band who looked for chinks of light in
everything. 'Here is a sunrise,' Love sang in the chorus.
'Ain't that enough?'

Gerry also said something that reminded me of my first
interview with Shirley: 'We don't travel as far as we think we
do from the music we like as children, really, do we? I still
like to keep in touch with the wee guy I was.' Of course,
Shirley had not written her songs, but she had remembered
them from her childhood, or hunted them down, sometimes
literally pulling them out of dust for others to hear them.
She had remembered the people who sung the songs before,
and made it her life's work to celebrate them, taking care as
she brought their voices back from the dead. She presented
music as a means of communion with ancestors — to not

sentimentalise or belittle them, but to try and accurately reflect who they were.

By the late 2000s, she was regularly giving lectures about female collectors like Lucy Broadwood, Ella May Leather and Mary Neal, and the Romany gypsy singers whose oral traditions were so often overlooked. And then in 2014, at seventy-eight, something incredible happened – Shirley started to sing again. She has released two beautiful albums since, *Lodestar* and *Heart's Ease*, in her new, older, richer, lovely vocals. She has performed live, had a film made about her, *The Ballad of Shirley Collins*, produced a second memoir, and expanded and reissued her first. I am hoping beyond hope that she records 'Gilderoy' again. One day I might even sing mine to her.

She remains one of the reasons why music makes me write: because I want to tell broader stories about the people that keep us going through the storms that life creates. I also want to stand before crowds, even when I find it unnerving to do so, trying to win them over to new melodies, new rhythms, new voices.

Track 9
Among Angels – Kate Bush

How Music Helps Us Heal

Thirty-six years. Four months. Out. Underground. Away from him, the little boy in the little blue blanket who had arrived in late April, his skin squishy like plasticine, his little head like fine glass. Away from her for a night, the frayed, manic figure dancing toe-to-toe in the kitchen in high summer, her brain galloping at a million miles an hour, her digital radio stuck to the Absolute '80s pop channel, stacked with smothering, familiar songs. She is trying to propel joy into the rhythms spiking around the room, into the dead air she inhales-exhales.

Away from the woman trying to hold on, I was now a woman throwing herself into the hot shell of the Piccadilly Line, trying to remember her younger, solid self; a self beyond my child, or even the idea of small children, that dissolved when I tried to reach out for it. An email had arrived from America, asking me to review a gig, and not just any gig. I grabbed at the opportunity to run away to West London, to wrest familiar experiences and sensations out of the air.

The US music website Pitchfork had asked me to review Kate Bush's first concert in thirty-five years at the Eventim Apollo, formerly the Hammersmith Odeon – a venue she'd last played on her only other tour, 1979's Tour of Life, when she was twenty. In that gig, she'd pioneered the use of the wireless headset, allowing her to dance and move freely as she sang. She had used mimes, magicians, back projections and constant costume changes to turn her ambitious pop into ambitious theatre. It was a venue she'd first been inside six years earlier, when she was four weeks shy of fifteen, watching David Bowie in his show as Ziggy Stardust, the night he announced his retirement. Bush talked about the power of that night in *Mojo* magazine in 2007: 'The atmosphere was just so charged that at the end, when he cried, we all cried with him.'

The pre-gig anticipation for the 2014 shows was just as extreme. Weepy hyperbole was being tossed around social media platforms before she had even turned up in the green room. But I didn't feel anything when I left the house that night. The journey felt alien. I felt the distance between me and my son stretching, as if the Tube was a fraying umbilical cord. I sat in the pub opposite the venue, a gin and tonic untouched in my hand, feeling outside my body, as if I was observing myself at a distance.

I came round to find myself facing the Apollo stage, not understanding how I'd got there. I can't remember ever feeling more isolated, watching the seats fill, the room rally, the crowds whoop and cheer.

*

In the first four months of my son's life, when I was struggling with what I thought was post-natal depression, the music that I clung to came from my childhood. The song that meant most to me was Yazz and the Plastic Population's 1988 cover of 'The Only Way Is Up'. I'd use its opening sirens, sampled from Sharon Redd's 1982 club hit 'Beat the Street', to blast me awake. The rest of the track would lap through the room in warm waves, sounding protective, amniotic; its running-on-the-spot rhythm, its gurgling

Roland 303 bass synthesiser, were things I'd known well for so long, unlike the current state I was in. I played it to feel each element trembling through layers of skin, surging through my arteries and valves. We'd been broken down, I sang to my boy. Hold on, hold on.

I first loved it when I was a few months off ten – its lyrics were in my first *Smash Hits* – and I'm sure I was drawn to it because the duo that made it, Coldcut, included samples of children's records in their songs. Matt Black had soldered his first synthesiser together at thirteen, following instructions from *Practical Electronics* magazine. Jon More was a DJ on pirate station Kiss FM and sold records at Reckless in Soho. Their first white-label track, 'Say Kids, What Time Is It?', came from a phrase in the fifties kids' show *Howdy Doody*, and sampled at least thirty-five other recordings. 'Doctorin' the House' used 'Say kids, what time is it?' again, alongside snippets from a 1966 DC Comics LP, including a phrase I loved rolling around my tongue, about a 'wicked plastic man'.

Other house acts followed their lead. S'Express sampled a 1976 record about the making of *Star Trek* for 'Theme for S'Express' ('enjoy this trip . . . 'cos it is a trip'). Bomb The Bass cut up an old Thunderbirds album for 'Beat Dis' ('keep this frequency clear . . . Thunderbirds are Go!'). I realise the appeal of British house records is partly about the industrial rhythms – about the clanking sounds of modern life given a structure and pulse – but I believe it's also about the reanimation of a collective childhood memory bank. Bands like Boards of Canada would do woozier things with children's voices nearer the end of the century, warping and stretching clips of speech from *Sesame Street* for tracks like

'The Color of Fire' and the rainbow-themed 'Roygbiv'. But in the early days of house music's heady bricolage, nostalgia and innocence were king. Its fans found escape in unsullied instincts and urges from simpler times.

And of course, my childhood had not been simple as such. But music had made it feel like it could be occasionally, offering me moments of playfulness and gleeful absurdity.

'The Only Way Is Up', like 'Doctorin' the House', was also sung by Yazz, a singer whose cool, soft voice felt full of grace. It made me feel held and embraced, and the song as a whole has always felt like a set of rungs for me to grip on to – I remember being shocked, as late as 2004, to find out it was a cover of a 1980 single by Otis Clay, which had done well in Northern Soul clubs. The 1988 version felt so complete to me that I couldn't believe its foundations had been lifted from elsewhere. But robust foundations for anything in life, I was finding back then, remained rare.

As a new parent, I hung on to songs that spoke to who I had been as a child, but I wanted my son to be different to her, though: less anxious, less nervous, stronger. I also knew that burying into nostalgia offered me comfort, but it wouldn't fix things. Going back into the past meant losing myself in constantly dislocating memories, and reminders of the parent who wasn't here to watch me parent. Dad had been in my mind often throughout my pregnancy, especially when it was coming to the end.

Hospitals always make me think of him. The long plastic corridors in Morriston Hospital used to loom large in my mind when I was young, like the tunnels that were attached to Elliott's house in *E.T.*, when E.T. was dying, about to be taken away by the authorities. I would hear my father in the bleep of the machines, in the musicality of them. I was in hospital for three days before my son was born, and I barely listened to music in those hours. I wanted to hear Dad there with me.

I forgot about him only for a while, in the labour room, a cannula in one hand, my husband's hand in the other, syntocin being dripped into my body to try and force the baby to come, as Beach House's 2010 album *Teen Dream* played through a small speaker on the end of the bed. It was a record I'd loved for four years at that point – we'd chosen it because it sounded beautiful and dream-like, full of wonder, a wonder that I hoped would accompany the new life still stuck in my non-behaving body.

My father returned in the darkness of the early Monday morning in the soft whooshes of the heartbeat print-out machine. He got louder when I was told that my baby's heart rate had started to fall, when the emergency paperwork was produced, when the anaesthetist asked if I was related to anyone who had died in an operating theatre. Louder when we realised that my mother would have to be called to find out if she knew if the anaesthetic had killed him. Louder still when I lay on a table in a white room, etherised from the lower spine down, strange creatures in sea-blue and sea-green fluttering around me like drowsy dragonflies.

I felt tugs and jabs somewhere both outside me and inside me, within a smile-shaped slash in my abdomen, as the surgeons resorted to forceps to pull a stuck, weary baby into the world. The midwife wouldn't tell us if the baby was OK, and then for a brief moment he was placed on my chest, before I was taken into recovery. I was told my husband and my baby would follow me straightaway. I was taken to a side ward, alone, and didn't see either of them for the next hour. It felt like a whole life.

We spent the next week in hospital, then the sleep deprivation hit, then the visions began.

The sound of my father was still there as I stood in the hospital lift, a week after I had given birth, when we were given the all-clear. The baby was OK. I was deemed to be OK. But I wasn't. It felt strange that I was being allowed to go home, to be alive.

*

Before my father returned firmly in my mind, I'd used music to ease me through my pregnancies. The night after I first found out that a tiny egg was embedding itself into the wall of my womb, I went to see the American electronic musician Keith Fullerton Whitman. I soaked into the dense, endless drones of the synthesisers, holding my husband's hand. Music was taking me out of my body, happily elsewhere.

A few weeks later, I saw Kraftwerk twice at Tate Modern, reviewed a Justin Timberlake secret gig just after he'd won a Brit Award, and was preparing for the biggest interview of my life by listening to songs from The Beatles' first album, *Please Please Me*. I folded myself into 'Do You Want to Know a Secret?', a song I knew from a compilation my mother played in the car when I was young – one of the few pop cassettes of hers that I remember. I felt excited to lose myself in the song and my work, in places that offered stimulation and security, when everything else felt out of my control.

A few days before the biggest interview of my life, I noticed a few spots of blood in my underwear. (It's common, don't worry, said a nurse the next day at the hospital, just something to keep an eye on.) Five minutes before the phone was due to ring for the biggest interview of my life, I went into the bathroom, and saw blood of two kinds: the first sharp and red, a horror-slick of brightness. The second was thick, congealing, purple-brown, soil, matter, decay.

I remember looking at myself in the mirror, washing my hands, going to my desk, the phone ringing, and hearing bone-deep Scouse vowels that I had listened to all my life. Interviewing Paul McCartney would have knocked me down clean on any ordinary day, especially when I heard him addressing me by name — a name he laughed at sweetly, half-sung, as he said it.

The twenty minutes felt like an out-of-body experience. Here was a voice I'd known so well in his Beatles compositions, on his solo tracks, on a song that had got to number one in mid-January 1984. My voice on my transcription tape is thin and translucent, a shadow of a voice, trying not to disappear.

Four nights later, in the ladies' bathroom in the Heavenly Social, one of my favourite music venues in London, four days after the scan that confirmed what we already knew, something grey fell out of me. It was a small sliver of matter, like overcooked liver. It was done. I remember going back through to the bar, hearing Pavement's 'Shady Lane' playing over the speakers. It's funny how that song has stuck in my mind. I let it consume me, absorb the numbness.

The next week, I wrote up my Paul McCartney interview, and two weeks later saw it on the cover of Q magazine. In the next few months, I went to lots of concerts, obliterating myself with drink, the love of friends, the love of being part of something outside myself. That July, another set of nerve cells and limb buds arrived, and this time, they settled in.

At sixteen weeks, we heard the foetal heartbeat for the first time, a regular, insistent 140 beats-per-minute. I went online as soon as I could and searched for songs: he was 'Call Me' by Blondie. In my third trimester, I threw myself into work, to save money for the months I wanted to take off to spend time with him. Work helped too because he was quiet, and I needed to be occupied away from worrying about him. Some days, he would barely move. Our local hospital became a regular destination, so I could hear that pulse, that pacy rhythm, fast, firm and steady.

I interviewed Kim Wilde and Kylie Minogue in those months, going back to Minogue's first performance of 'I Should Be So Lucky' on *Top of the Pops*, recorded in Sydney in a convertible car, her hair flying in the breeze, so young and carefree, enjoying old Wilde songs like 'You Came', consoling myself in innocent, immaculately polished pop. When I interviewed Damon Albarn at his studio near the Westway, he got his comfiest chair out for the woman with the fully occupied belly. He also let me nose among his instruments, including an old electric organ like one at my grandma's, which lived in the room in which Grandpa died. Damon told me how melancholic he thought Welsh hymns were. Each note he pressed on the keyboard opened a door into an old semi-detached house, unlocked another image of a woman in her mid-fifties singing to a little girl.

I also filled those last months with gigs because our baby responded to loud music. He first wriggled to his dad's band, The Drink, in a basement venue in Dalston. He went so crazy to Beyoncé at the O2 that I wrapped a cardigan around my middle, a woolly alternative to ear defenders. I saw Suede at the Royal Albert Hall two weeks before he was due, with my regular gig-friend Stuart alongside me, who, importantly, had helped deliver his son at home. Stuart's only duties that night were propping me up as the band played 'Still Life', 'The Living Dead', 'New Generation', 'Stay Together', as the audience stood on their feet, and I wobbled on mine. I felt my anxieties buzz along with Mat Osman's basslines, but he also converted them into something distinct and triumphant. For one evening, I was so young, so gone.

The only music I can't listen to from that time any more is the Beach House record. It now sounds to me like a set of warped lullabies, the opening notes of its first track, 'Zebra', falling gently from the speakers like raindrops in a nursery rhyme, before they hit the floor and burn. The soft, misty jangle of 'Norway' now sounds like a child's breath collecting and dispersing on a window pane, just the once, never to be seen again. Victoria Legrand's unconventional, deep voice was meant to sound like it was coming in and out of focus on the record, but it is now the seep of drugs into my hand, reminding me that he had to arrive quickly, and that I couldn't make him do that on my own.

In the seven days we were kept in the ward, I listened to hardly any music as this quiet, small person slowly emerged into life. I couldn't fill the silence that surrounded me with sound or with meaning. Later, I had flashbacks to some of those moments in the hospital — to the theatre, to the shoulder-shrugging midwife, to the ward where I waited so long for my son to come back to me – and years later, I realised I'd been suffering post-traumatic stress. It didn't help that I felt my first function as a parent – to bring him into the world – had been so fraught with concern. Back then, I needed to be kind to myself, and get better. I also needed someone to soothe me, to sing to me, to tell me what to do.

*

In early 2019, I read *The Book You Wish Your Parents Had Read (and Your Children Will Be Glad That You Did)* by psychotherapist Philippa Perry. It made me think a lot about my son's early years, and how I behaved during them. 'Having a child of your own can trigger any feelings you dissociated from as a child,' came one of her statements, like a lightning bolt. 'They may be uncomfortable, disconcerting, distracting and strange.' She later added: 'whatever age your child is, they are liable to remind you, on a bodily level, of the emotions you went through when you were at a similar age . . . [you] won't remember consciously what it's like to be a baby, but on other levels, you will remember, and your child will keep reminding you'.

I didn't want to unleash any sadness into his life. In those early months, snapshots from his birth and that first week in hospital kept returning to me like phantoms, scorched with static, like terrifying freeze-frames. I thought allowing myself to be far away and alone in an environment I knew well would be helpful. At first, it had the opposite effect, but then, after an hour at the Kate Bush gig, everything started to spin, eddy and change.

A song came along in the Eventim Apollo that night that helped me heal. It did something to me just like music did to Perry, who talked about its power perfectly on Radio 3's *Private Passions* programme. '[Music] can touch a place inside us that really resonates, that we might not have been able to put into words,' she told Michael Berkeley. 'We can feel along to the music, and recognise our feelings, even if we haven't got words for those feelings. This could be part of the reason why music is so important to people, because it just seems to wash over you, or get into you, in a way that seems to hold and understand you.'

It was a bit like having a hug with someone, she added. 'You might have a wordless hug with somebody, and it might mean different things to both of you, but you might both come away feeling held and understood.' So we might. So I would.

The song came along right at the end of the concert. Three hours earlier, I had wanted someone to steady me, hold my hand, at the same time as I wanted to ignore all the critics I knew, from the *Guardian*, *Times*, *Daily Mail*, all of them energised, ready to write up their reviews for their papers' 10.30 p.m. deadlines. For the first time in my professional life, I felt utterly unlike them. I didn't want to be swept up in the wave of exultation consuming the room. I expected everyone else would give the concert five stars. I wanted to acknowledge that Kate wasn't superhuman, like I wasn't superhuman.

Then suddenly there she was with her band. Older, her hair piled on top of her head, a normal human being. Three thousand voices crested in a wailing tide of sound. Her group played six songs, straight and direct, including the first ever live performances of 'Hounds of Love' and 'Running Up That Hill (A Deal With God)'. Bush's voice occasionally wavered, but it was still a lovely, shivering thing. Something for me didn't click though. I felt disappointed, too far gone for these beautiful songs to have any redemptive power.

Then came the last section of 'King of the Mountain', Kate's comeback single from 2005. It imagined what it would have been like to be Elvis Presley, and what he would be doing if he were still alive. Kate was singing about the wind whistling, when one of her band came to the front of the stage. He swung a rope around his head, then the music stuck, jarred, repeated itself in a huge cacophony of sound. Smoke and yellow paper were suddenly cannoning through the air – I picked up one of the pieces of paper, and on it was a quote from Tennyson's 'The Coming of Arthur', the poem that inspired her suite of songs 'The Ninth Wave', on the second side of 1985's *Hounds of Love*, my favourite Kate Bush album. And then came her voice – 'little light, shining' – and 'The Ninth Wave' rushed in, the story of a woman lost at sea, brought to life on a stage turning into a whale's mouth. I found myself staring at projections of waves, steampunk dancers spinning like whirlpools, and an image of Kate surrounded by water in her lifejacket, fighting to swim.

In the song 'Watching You Without Me', Kate appeared at the edge of a small part of the set, like a ghost in the family home, watching a man and a boy. The boy was her son in real life, Bertie, then sixteen. She sang that she should have been home hours ago. She despaired that he couldn't hear her. Then in the second half of the show, she performed 'A Sky of Honey', the long suite of songs from the second side of 2005's *Aerial*, which follows the movement of an ordinary day. The original album began with Bertie, seven at the time of its recording, saying his first words: 'Mummy, Daddy, the day is full of birds.' Tonight, the concert programme revealed he was the reason for his mother's return to performance.

'A Sky of Honey' was another theatrical production, unfurling around a wooden mannequin of a young boy being led around the stage by a puppeteer. I watched him being trapped in a mythic landscape, then by stabs of pain and flashes of stark, dramatic light; I couldn't fully comprehend the narrative unfolding, but it didn't matter. I knew there was something subliminal and powerful being shared here about the bond between mothers and sons.

I watched Kate playing the piano for some of it, alone, unable to help him. I remember feeling something inside me slip from its moorings. I wanted to protect him always, but I couldn't. I wanted to be everything for him, but I wouldn't. It was then that the tears came, and Kate came back for her encore, on her own again, with her piano. The room was held in a silence that felt expectant, longing. And then she sang.

For a moment, it felt like she was only singing to me.

'Only you . . .' soared her voice.

I felt myself in her breaths.

'. . . Can do something about it.'

*

'Among Angels' is the last song on Bush's 2011 album *50 Words for Snow*, a record consisting of seven tracks which explore different moments, both icy and cosy, of winter. I'd reviewed the album for the BBC three years earlier, but almost forgotten it existed. In the first verse of its final song, Kate sings like a kind deity offering advice, then emerges as a helpful observer.

It is a quiet song, lifted by delicate touches of single piano keys, and then soft, unusual chords. It addresses someone who says that they 'fall apart' – not someone who says they are *falling apart*, which suggests a one-time-only, dramatic experience. The fall here seemed to be a frequent, repeated action, which was something I understood.

Kate's narrator then said she 'might understand' what that person meant by that act, which was a sensitive line. It gave that person space to have their own feelings aside from hers. Then she added, 'Aren't we all the same?', broadening her empathy, 'In and out of doubt.' I felt Kate as a narrator disappear, and willed her to be expressing these sentiments from a place of personal understanding, to pull me in.

Then her visions began. She could 'see angels' surrounding that person, even though that person didn't know they were there. These apparitions could carry you, she said, allow you to rest in their hands. While they do this, they 'shimmer like mirrors in summer'. I saw my reflections in them.

Then Kate told me there was someone who had loved me for ever, 'but you don't know it'.

More tears came then. I knew I was drawing my own loss out of her words, but I sensed everyone around me being caught in that moment. I looked around for the first time – everyone I could see was glassy-eyed, lost in the moment, in awe. It was as if I was at one with everyone else in the room in the release of those tears: it was an extraordinary feeling, full of vulnerability, and the acceptance of it, of its strength. In the weeks that followed, I would take a message from those words, use them as part of my recovery. It was like something finally connected: I could let my father support me – and still appear, shining – but I could also carry on with my life.

After 'Among Angels', Kate sang another song from *Hounds of Love*, 'Cloudbusting', which now felt euphoric. It reminded me of her playing a little boy in its video, helping her father, played by Donald Sutherland. She was Peter; he was the psychoanalyst and inventor Wilhelm Reich. Together, they pointed a cloudbusting machine to the skies, trying to harness a universal life force to create rain, to create miracles.

I returned to 'Among Angels' when my son was sleeping, closing my eyes, breathing, starting to feel better. At the time, I thought it was because I had connected to Kate all on my own; I realised soon after it was something much deeper, more profound. I had connected to her on an intimate, emotional level, at the same time as other people did, in their own ways – it was like the experience of dancing to Kraftwerk at Tribal Gathering but both inverted and broadened. As an experience, it was quiet not loud. It involved being seated and settled, not standing. It was about a vibration moving through our seats in the room, pulsing with a subtle but unshakeable intensity.

*

In the years since that almost spiritual moment, I've thought often about how music can repair us as parents and as people. I came across a project online called Music For Healing by

Richard Norris, a musician whose explorations into different genres and productions I'd always found fascinating. He'd been part of the Beyond the Wizard's Sleeve project (I'd loved their psychedelic 'reanimations' of favourite tracks by Midlake, Franz Ferdinand and Simian Mobile Disco) and a member of The Grid with Soft Cell's Dave Ball (who had huge dance hits in the nineties, like the ridiculously catchy, banjo-driven 'Swamp Thing'). Now he was creating long ambient pieces to help listeners help themselves. He began making music like this after moving back to West London. Drug-dealing gangs were hanging out in his doorway and wouldn't let him pass, and his female next-door neighbours moved out because they were being constantly harassed. 'I didn't feel safe at all in the place I was meant to feel safe,' he explains, one afternoon on the phone. 'I needed to create a safe space of my own.'

Norris had always found refuge in music. In his mid-teens, he worked in a local market, where he would play and replay a tape of sixties classic soul tracks through his headphones. 'It gave me this feeling in my heart. It was almost as powerful as puberty, almost: "Oh, my God! That's what soul music is about. It's the soul!"' On a holiday in his twenties, he remembers playing Brian Eno's *On Land* on repeat for two weeks. 'Those pieces just did something to me – they somehow gave me this kind of massive release of tension.' He thinks that the situation in which we play songs, and the associations we carry with them ever after, help too. 'In other words, I now associate *On Land* with sitting on a sun lounger.'

I tell him about my experience with 'Among Angels', and how it hit me on that night in 2014. I tell him how

I've dug into it ever since, with my eyes shut, to access the same feeling. He gets it: he has a similarly close relationship to Éliane Radigue's astonishing *Trilogie De La Mort*, a work of three long drone-based compositions, influenced by the Tibetan Book of the Dead. 'First, when your brain's concentrating on one thing, it's probably cutting off something else, isn't it?' He introduces his interest in meditation, which he has practised for years, and how deeper states have helped fine-tune his focus. Then he talks about the power of an individual closing in on musical details, especially when they're in a crowd. 'I always found it amazing that when I started doing my meditations with, say, seventeen other people, suddenly it felt stronger. I've always been interested in why that is. And I felt that same feeling seeing Brian Wilson doing *Smile* at the Royal Festival Hall [in 2004]. No one knew if he could do it – it was amazing that he was actually performing it really – and you could almost see the kind of feeling in the air.' That combination of not believing that something was happening while it was actually happening, I say, could be said of my Kate Bush night too. 'Yes! It's the power of people just willing someone to do something.'

Norris mentions the artist Rupert Sheldrake's theory of morphic resonance: the idea of mysterious, telepathic interconnections between organisms and collective memories within species. I read later that Sheldrake's theory is considered pseudoscience by many scholars, but its principles resonate with Norris's personal experiences. He then offers an analogy connected to nature that works for me regardless, that feels profound in its beauty. 'In those meditations, and that gig, it felt like we were part of a murmuration, when all the birds are all doing the same thing at the same time.'

Norris has made his own pieces using the same principles for the Music For Healing project, posting them online, hoping people will gather around them in the same way – which they have done since early 2020. 'It was lovely – it wasn't just one person writing in, it was loads of people writing in. They were all saying kind of the same thing: This is really helping with my anxieties. It's helping with my mental health.' He's recently worked with an NHS Trust in York, who ran a trial in which music was actually prescribed: the results, anecdotally, were strong, but hard to assess using conventional scientific methods because of other variables in the mix, like how the act of sitting and resting on its own could help people to feel better.

Norris doesn't mind though. 'The thing we were really looking for on that project was just to give people a kind of licence to listen like that. If music is prescribed by a doctor and they say, "Do this," people go, "Well, the doctor's said that," and that helps.' For him, all the proof he needed was that people communicated with him, that they flocked together, and found comfort in each other. It's been one of the best musical experiences of his life, he says, and then he laughs. 'Even better than being on *Top of the Pops*.'

*

In her 2015 book *The Music of Being*, music therapist Alison Levinge discusses how parents and children often find support in a musical world:

As human beings, we are conceived in a musically orien-
tated environment and our development is formed within a
context of different musical elements. Observing a mother
with her young baby, we see many musical qualities reflected
in how they communicate with each other: the tempo and
rhythm of their to-and-fro interactions, the melodic shaping
of a mother's voice as she coos and babbles along with the
baby, or the emotional 'attunement' as she experiences the
different feelings that her baby evokes in her.

After that 'Among Angels' summer, as my baby began to
smile, sit up and physically respond, I started enjoying
music-making in groups. Baby sensory classes I'd attended
since he was tiny now started to make sense. I have a precious video of my pudgy ten-month-old wiggling a sparkly
blue pom-pom along to Boney M's 'Hooray! Hooray! It's
a Holi-Holi-Day', which I still play often. I love that I can
hear my laughter in the background.

I also sang to him. At bedtime, there were lullabies, like
'*Cysga Di Fy Mhlentyn Tlws*' ('Sleep You Now, My Pretty
Child'), a Welsh folk song that my grandmother had sung
to me. In the daytime, I'd sing The Beatles' 'Here Comes
the Sun', changing the words to 'Here comes my son', as
I saw his expressive face in his baby-walker slowly revolve
around the sofa.

I remember what Sandra Trehub of the Music Development Lab had said about babies not beginning life with 'a
blank musical slate', because of the melodies and rhythms
they had picked up in the womb. I hadn't thought about
how the knowledge of this is retained in new parents. In his
2005 book *The Singing Neanderthals*, anthropologist Simon

Mithen explains infant-directed speech – the way in which we talk to our children in sing-songy style, also known as IDS – in more detail. 'Human infants demonstrate an interest in and sensitivity to the rhythms, tempos and melodies of speech long before they are able to understand the meanings of words. In essence, the usual melodic and rhythmic features of spoken language – prosody – are highly exaggerated so that our utterances adopt an explicitly musical character.'

Another anthropologist with interests in the evolution of animal behaviour, Ellen Dissanayake, goes further in her analysis of IDS. She believed that its musical aspects evolved as a direct response to the helplessness of human infants, the least ready of the mammalian species to emerge into the living world. In an essay in the 2000 handbook of evolutionary biomusicology *The Origins of Music*, titled 'Antecedents of the Temporal Arts in Early Mother–Infant Interaction', she views music 'in its origins more broadly than vocalisations'. These vocalisations can't be separated from the facial and bodily movements that accompany them, in other words: they are more of a multidimensional activity where many interactions are melodiously tied together.

Unlike some, Dissanayake shies away from the evolutionary idea of music as a way to attract mates. Its power to charm is less important to her than its ability to coordinate different people's emotions, and promote what she calls 'conjoinment'. In this process, mother and baby recognise and respond to each other to create a music all of their own – and Dissanayake suggests this has even further potential. 'Mother–infant dialogue seems to be the prototype for a kind of fundamental emotional narrative that adult music, dance movement and poetic language grow out of, build upon, exemplify and sustain.'

*

I remember the first time I saw my son reacting to music without being in a class or being prompted. He was hanging on to our low-rise Ikea record shelves in the living room, moving himself around slowly, still not able to walk, and then suddenly he was jiggling his head to the Future Sounds of London's 'Papua New Guinea'. Oh, my delight – I jumped up and applauded. I also have a lovely video of him at three, wearing blue plaid pyjamas, chalking purple scribbles on his blackboard to a song that had just come on the radio, New Order's 'Blue Monday', his hips shifting to the beat in exact time, moving much more elegantly than I had when I was in my early twenties in London clubbing at Trash. We were sharing songs as parent and child without really noticing we were sharing them – and when we *were* noticing them, we were often singing and dancing along to them. Music was a means of us magically attaching, building our bond.

Then came the songs my son got obsessed with on his own. Talking Heads' 'Road to Nowhere' popped up one Sunday on a Spotify radio algorithm, while we were all eating a post-roast dinner apple crumble. He stopped mid-spoon-to-mouth. 'Again!' he said when it finished. Marching band rhythm. David Byrne's squeals and yelps. 'Again!' It is still known in our house, three years later, as the apple crumble song. I showed him the music video a while later, and he loved David Byrne's long-limbed human puppetry, and 'the bit where the old man goes in the box, Mummy, and comes out as a baby. How does he do that?' I told my son we're all the same people as we were when we were born, really. He looked at me as if I was mad. He then asked me to play the video again, kept yelping, kept dancing.

Recently, he's found his first favourite group on his own, a band whose songs I didn't care for when they were around: The Spice Girls. He listened to them with his female cousins on holiday, cousins who used to live nearby, but have since moved away. When he sings along to 'Stop!' or 'Say You'll Be There' in the car or demands that I tell him who's singing each line – Ginger's his favourite – I think I know what he's doing. He's trying to use music to feel close to other people, to enjoy how it makes him feel, to help find his place in the world. Music is helping him grow up, as it did me: it is helping me see who I was, and who the two of us could be. Parenting has also made me listen to songs again with fresh ears as I register his reactions. It turns them into new creatures. It's a beautiful thing.

Philippa Perry said something else on that episode of *Private Passions* on Radio 3, about what her only child had taught her. 'She brought me right back in the moment so that I could smell the flowers and enjoy the daisies and splash in a puddle and delight in that. She brought me back to my senses, really.'

My son sings in the back seat, happily, noisily. I'm giving you everything, all that joy can bring, yes I swear.

Track 10
April 5th – Talk Talk
Why We Grieve When Musicians Die

I was in the car when my phone rang, on a wet country lane, turning around the hedges, heading towards home. It was seven or so, early evening, in those heart-quickening weeks between winter and spring when the world is beginning again. Snowdrops suddenly appear like magical beings, offering up pale, curious heads. Daffodils then unfurl their butter-yellow collars, fluffing out their ruffs. The nights start to shake off all that thick, viscous ink, and the beautiful stuff is just around the corner. In these weeks, I always cling on to the light seeping into each day, every ray, every second.

That night, I glanced at the flashing phone on the passenger seat: LAURA SNAPES, it said. If it had begun with an 02920, it would have been BBC Wales, asking if I'd come on air to talk about why someone mattered to people, whether or not they mattered to me. If it was someone from the *Guardian*, particularly on their mobile phone, it was different. They had staff or contracted writers for the big and immediate news. If they called me, they were asking me to write something about someone who had died, someone whose music I loved.

I saw an entrance to a muddy farm track and manoeuvred my tyres over the bumpy ground, set the hazard lights to blink in the dusk. 'It's Mark Hollis,' Laura said. I sat in the car for five minutes – an orange husk in the twilight – then drove home, ran upstairs, kissed my son sleeping in his bed, and opened my laptop to see emotions distilled to sentences and hyperlinks on a screen. This was how Talk Talk's 'Life's

What You Make It' had changed my life. This is how *Spirit of Eden* helped me through. Then I opened Google and Rock's Backpages, read old interviews, wrote eight hundred words of yearning and longing, and pressed send.

How bizarre this is, I thought, the next morning, as I received private messages and public replies. Many said thank you, I felt the same way, now I want to share my own stories with you, a total stranger, about a man we didn't know and never met and never even saw live.

My copy of *The Colour of Spring*, Talk Talk's third album, my favourite of theirs, sat next to me on my desk. The brightly coloured moths on the cover had always looked simultaneously beautiful and aggressive to me, full of the wonder, strangeness and ferocity of nature, the dots on their wings staring at me like eyes, fixed and fierce, now in defiance of death.

Because pop music as we know it began in the mid-twentieth century, and the inevitability of human physical decline has not yet been magically reversed, we're now living at a time when pop stars keep dying. In some parts of the industry, especially those that are dictated by focus groups, sales sheets, statistical models and algorithms, pop stars are often expected to become more than living, breathing individuals. They are meant to be lifestyle ambassadors or brands with heartbeats and pulses, repositories of values to be positioned against the fluctuations of fashion and a record company's finances. But while the record labels might try their hardest, musicians don't achieve immortality.

The news that changed the rules for dead pop stars came early on a January morning in 2016. It came on the eleventh, as luck would have it for me, on the thirty-second anniversary of my father's death. I'd approached the anniversary confidently that year, with a new sense of positivity. It helped that my little boy was nearly two, no longer so helpless and vulnerable, and neither was I.

I remember turning on the radio later than usual, and David Bowie singing about Planet Earth being blue, but there being nothing we could do. I looked half-asleep at my phone – how weird – I had three missed calls from different BBC Radio networks, and an email from my editor at a women's pop culture website, The Pool. It wasn't yet seven-thirty. Shaun Keaveny repeated to the audience what he'd known since just before his show went on air, only half an hour earlier.

In a way, death was content and everyone wanted a piece of it, to offer their readers some explanation of what could happen to people who had always seemed bigger than us. I also felt my stories bursting through, and so my stories came out. I'd first loved Bowie as Jareth in *Labyrinth*, and not caring about being cool, this is what I wrote about for The Pool. Those sharp, mismatched eyes, that unusual voice, the crazy wig. And as I was nine, nearly ten: those trousers.

I thought about how we can forget how our favourite pop stars sometimes seemed incidental in our lives. In my teens, Bowie was a peripheral figure to me, nothing more than an odd presence in pop culture, a drum and bass-loving elder floating around *The Big Breakfast* and *Don't Forget Your Toothbrush*. Everything changed in my early twenties, when a Bowie singles collection CD bought second-hand from More Music in Swansea got me hooked. 'Rock 'n' Roll

Suicide' is still my first tiny London basement bedroom in the spring of 2000, all the dowelling-connected CD towers and wonky hanging rails and Bowie telling me I wasn't alone. 'Wild Is the Wind' is me wishing somebody would love-me-love-me-love-me. When Bowie began his set at Glastonbury with that song later that summer, right in front of me, in his frock coat and *Man Who Sold the World* ringlets, I considered it kismet. I saw a man who kept changing himself, and – as always – I wanted that facility too.

The second side of *Low* is Fritz Lang's *Metropolis*, my favourite film when I was twenty-two – my housemate Alex and I would turn the volume down on my DVD, put her vinyl copy on, loud, and let 'Warszawa' and 'Art Decade' take over. *Reality* is showing it to a boy I had kissed for the first time only three days earlier. That boy is now my husband. 'Where Are We Now?' is me getting caught up in the magic of its being released at all, but also in its exquisite sadness, its acknowledgement of the passing of time, its acquiescence to those cold, hard facts of life.

Blackstar is me listening to it on the afternoon of its release, the day of Bowie's sixty-ninth birthday, and its mood feeling too much, too cavernous, for where I wanted to be. I had already heard 'Lazarus', following its single release before Christmas, a little too often. I'd loved its opening Joy Division-echoing bassline, and the slow, doleful sighs of Donny McCaslin's saxophone. By January, I needed something brighter.

Two days later, Bowie was dead, on the tenth of January in New York; the news filtered through to the UK in the early morning of the eleventh. Crowds were clustering in Brixton,

I heard, leaving flowers; I was on the other side of London, having a day off with my toddler. I stayed riveted to BBC 6 Music for hours, playing at home with my son, and talked about the experience a few days later for the *Guardian*. It was like we were all gathering in a virtual wake. I spoke to Shaun Keaveny about the experience of being bombarded with tweets, texts and emails. 'It was like being in Central Park when Lennon died,' he said, 'all these people flocking to one place.' Except this place was no-place, online.

For me, Shaun was also the first person to pin down why Bowie's death mattered. 'Bowie's music reminds you of a point in your life when new ideas start to open up for you, so here came these people talking about songs that reminded them of times they had lost, and people they had lost.' Then he offered me a bloody stab of reality. 'It reminds you you're going to die too, doesn't it?'

*

A few weeks after Bowie died, Brendan O'Neill, editor of Spiked Online, wrote a piece that criticised public expressions of grief. He did so by throwing himself onto the Oxford English Dictionary, the first resort of the person thinking they're beginning an essay with a marvellous rhetorical flourish, even though they're not. 'Grief is physical and mental pain. It's oppression. It is, in the words of the OED, "hardship, suffering, injury". To feel grief is to feel "pained, oppressed". Are these Bowie fans suffering? Really suffering? No, they aren't. They're sad.'

The trouble was, I worried that this professional contrarian was right. At the same time, I knew how bruised I felt after the news of Bowie's death. I noticed how much time I was spending messaging friends – as well as complete strangers on social media – about elements of his life, dissecting lyrics, old interviews, music videos and performances. In a 2017 essay, 'Grief, Commiseration and Consumption following the Death of a Celebrity', American academics Scott K. Radfor and Peter H. Bloch would investigate how audio, video and online technologies have amplified this intensity. 'The difference [today],' they concluded, 'is that people generally no longer struggle to find others who understood their interest and devotion.'

Still, it struck me that friends who felt the news with a similar weight to me had also experienced sudden, devastating bereavements. I wondered if Bowie's death was acting like a macabre funfair mirror, magnifying and twisting the memories of other losses in our lives.

I reacted to how I felt by writing more about Bowie. I wrote a piece for the *Guardian* digging into the secret messages being debated online around the lyrics and cover art and music of *Blackstar*. The title was another name for a cancer lesion, the title of an Elvis Presley song about death, and its release date was the inception date of the replicant Roy Batty in *Blade Runner*, one of Bowie's favourite films. The mention of 'Ormen' in the title track referred to a village where Bowie's old girlfriend, Hermione Farthingale, had gone to make a film in 1969, *Song of Norway*, and Bowie had worn a T-shirt with these words on it for the video to 'Where Are We Now?'. I bought one soon after. I was exploring wormholes within wormholes.

Later in 2016, I wrote about Bowie's involvement with the TV film of Raymond Briggs's *The Snowman*: another appearance of his in my childhood which people of my generation still watched as we had our own children. I also wrote about feelings of public grief for The Quietus, wondering if deaths of distant people weigh more in our lives because we live in times which feel increasingly dislocated and dislodged. I also wondered whether the horrors of 2016 (hello Brexit, hello Trump) made us want to communicate more restlessly, urgently, intensely with ideas we believed in.

I wrote about the place where these musicians have always existed: in the life of the mind, which just happens to be where grief exists too. Grief is about 'a communication of ideas and feelings,' I wrote, 'a dialogue suddenly stopping, becoming a monologue when you didn't want it to.' I said grief was the process of wanting to share more and be more with people who are no longer here, and I still believe that. Music gives us a path to them, and at the same time it appears to sit outside mortality, offering us songs which, when we want them to, appear frozen in time.

*

Recently, I found out about a blog written in 2016 by the psychologist Fiona Murden, author of the 2020 book *Mirror Thinking: How Role Models Make Us Human*. She wrote the blog after more sudden deaths of pop stars followed Bowie's, including Prince in April, who was fifty-seven, and George Michael, my beloved childhood favourite, on Christmas Day, at fifty-three. (I remember a message coming late on Christmas Day to talk about his death on the radio and turning it down: I remember thinking, I can't be the woman who just churns out paragraphs on dead pop stars. I also need this Baileys-fuelled wake with my sister-in-law in the kitchen right now, singing 'Praying for Time', 'A Different Corner' and 'Jesus to a Child'.)

Murden began her blog, 'Sorry You Are Gone', by mentioning people to whom she had been close who had died in her life: a little girl she used to babysit, her late father. 'Grief is an odd and complex emotion which I've found to be strangely different with every relationship lost,' she began. She then discussed the deaths of musicians, and why they matter to us, even though we weren't known by the people who died. '[They] represent another form of relationship and a different type of grief.'

And although these relationships with pop stars are one-sided, 'or what is technically known as "parasocial"', she continued, 'they are ever-present in our lives, defining elements of who we are: our values, beliefs, attitudes, in the same way as our friends do'. She admitted feeling shock when Prince died, whom she had seen live in concert, although she only owned a few of his albums. 'I never glorified Prince, so why did I feel grief? [Because] grief is the normal and natural reaction to loss or change of any kind.'

Prince was a musician whose songs she had valued – which is as important as loving them, she said – from early on in her life. In her common room at school, Prince was played 'at any given opportunity', his sexuality and graphic lyrics offering her and her friends a sense of forbidden excitement that 'undoubtedly influenced our self-image'. As a rebellious role model, he held values and character traits that Murden and her friends were eager to absorb; his prolific output also meant his status as an artist never waned as they got older.

Murden also loved how he defied norms and expectations, creating a degree of mystique around his work that
kept him incredibly seductive. '[He] represented a web of
relationships from school through to family. This mirrors
the death of someone we love; someone who holds people
together and also preserves elements of our past that form
our identity.'

I speak to Murden on an April afternoon, telling her how
I'd loved sharing songs from Bowie's life with friends on
email after he'd died, and with strangers on social media.
She did too. '[Music] always has this sense of belonging
about it, because we know, somewhere out there, there are
other people listening to it, or that have listened to it, too.
Always, at a very primitive level, we feel connected to other
people through it, even if we don't know who they are.'

She is also interested in how we try to recreate stories
about people after they die, and how social media helps
this along. 'I mean, that's how we exist, and it's how we've
existed for generations, isn't it? You think about it in an
even longer timeframe than that – how humans have been
around in a blink of an eyelid, basically, in terms of time
– and for so long we couldn't write, we couldn't read. We
transmitted information through stories. If I'm looking at it
as a psychologist, our personal narrative is absolutely crucial
to holding our personal identity together, and our sense
of self-worth and our sense of understanding of where we
fit in. Hearing other people's stories allows us to place our
own story.'

And then into that mix in the particular situation I'm
describing, I say, songs come along. 'And songs tell stories
too, don't they? And on top of that, you've got the emotion

that's transmitted by music, which is incredibly powerful. The beat and the rhythm and the collective understanding.'

After speaking to Murden, I thought about the number of music documentaries and monthly magazine covers dominated by the dead, and how long mortality has been a defining element of rock and roll lore. Its early mystique was driven by the accidental deaths of young people in the air or on the road, like Eddie Cochran, Patsy Cline and Otis Redding, as well as the three musicians who crashed to earth on 'the day the music died'. Then came the deaths by misadventure, of the likes of Janis Joplin, Jimi Hendrix and Jim Morrison, the murders of Sam Cooke, John Lennon and Marvin Gaye, and the sad stories of artists whose potential was cut short by debilitating illness: Tammi Terrell and Bob Marley with cancer, Karen Carpenter with anorexia, Patrick Cowley, Sylvester and so many others with AIDS. The reputations of these musicians and so many others became frozen in their interrupted adulthood, captured in unachieved potential; their pliable images, not their bodies, achieved immortality.

Dead pop stars also allow easy opportunities to make money, of course, and editorially, they're simple subjects to deal with: not only can you not libel the dead, but they won't answer back. They are also means of strengthening communities of devotion, but these communities then grow around an absence that is unable to interject, reply or rebut in any conversations, and this troubles me, given what it says about our relationship to musicians when they are living. '[Death] can see an artist elevated, celebrated and validated in ways they never were in life,' writes Eamonn Forde in *Leaving the Building: The Lucrative Afterlife of Music Estates*, a huge book which digs into what happens to the recorded output and musical legacies of these people.

Forde writes that public grief after the death of popular musicians is not a new phenomenon. Quoting Philip Norman's 1996 biography of Buddy Holly, he recounts that in schools throughout America and Britain, whole classes turned up for lessons 'wearing black armbands'. This happened in America even though Holly's last single before his death, 'It Doesn't Matter Anymore', was a flop. After his death, it climbed the charts, its lyrics about a couple going off in different directions, and it not mattering at all, gaining new mournful meanings.

Forde also cites Dave Laing's 1971 biography of Holly to show how musicians' deaths are often felt more powerfully than those of artists working in other fields: 'The death in mid-career of a singer . . . has a more dramatic effect than that of a writer, painter or director; because they are performers, people with an immediate physical presence for their audience.' Music 'released for the first time after their death' is also given 'a new significance'. A voice is singing from the grave, eerily alive, full of breath, articulation and expression.

And then there are records released just before an artist's death. *Blackstar* had a different life for two days. Leonard Cohen's last album, *You Want It Darker*, had seventeen. The commentary about it on release included details about Cohen's ill-health — which had been made known by his family — about his severe mobility issues, about him being confined to his daughter's house, as he recorded its songs with his son, Adam. 'Occasionally, in bouts of joy, he would even, through his pain, stand up in front of the speakers,'

Adam told *Rolling Stone* magazine. We knew he was not long for this world, and how sad that was, but his album, full of blackly comic ruminations on death and life, revealed he was happy to tell us about it, suggesting he was ready to go.

We don't know if Bowie was. We assume he was not. But 'in death, as in life', as Forde says, 'Bowie was a trailblazer'. He left a perfectly planned will, ensuring that his wife Iman, and children Duncan and Lexi, would be looked after as he wished. He also managed to keep his personal life private while making an album that would help people talk about death, as he approached his.

*

Palliative care doctor Mark Taubert did not expect someone to write a piece of music inspired by something he had done in his work. After all, in January 2016 he was a consultant in a hospital in Cardiff, looking after the dying, trying to do his annual appraisal around his shifts. But when he sat down to write it, he couldn't stop thinking about a patient he had just met in hospital that Monday. 'She just said, have you heard that David Bowie has died? At first I felt, how strange – it felt like such an unusual thing to talk about when we'd first met.' Mark is a huge music fan, a lover of Bowie, Nick Cave, Mogwai, Bauhaus and The Doors among others. 'We had met to talk about how her cancer had spread and that it was not curable. But I said yes, I have heard about it, and then I asked her what her favourite tunes were, and it was such a fantastic moment.'

I first spoke to Taubert online, after we had both attended a Nick Cave gig at Cardiff's Millennium Centre; we later meet at the cancer centre where he works, his directness and kindness shining through. That gig was billed 'Conversations with Nick Cave', inspired by a regular newsletter the artist wrote to fans called *The Red Hand Files*, answering all manner of questions about life and death, as well as matters more mundane. Cave had started writing it after his son, Arthur, died at fifteen, after falling from a cliff in East Sussex. Sensitively, Mark had asked Nick what music he would like to have playing when he died, as he often asked his patients at work. Cave was quiet, and then he said, nothing. He'd want silence.

In his palliative care practice, Mark had found more people gravitating towards songs when he asked them that question – and his conversation with the woman that Monday had underlined how readily people would speak about music. Later that week, in his office, he found himself writing about her to David Bowie, in the form of a letter. 'We discussed your death and your music, and it got us talking about numerous weighty subjects, that are not always straightforward to discuss. In fact, your story became a way for us to communicate very openly about death, something many doctors and nurses struggle to introduce as a topic of conversation.' He kept going. He added his reflections on *Blackstar*, saying what Bowie made in the time leading up to his death had had a profound effect on him and the people he worked with. 'And then I went, wow, this is getting quite long now and is probably inappropriate for my appraisal folder.'

Mark tells me about being brought up in what then was West Germany. He remembers reading about Bowie's famous 1987 concert near the Reichstag in West Berlin, and it being so loud that crowds of East Germans gathered on the other side. He remembers listening to him while living in Cologne and then studying at Dundee. 'You know, you can have dates to mark the stations of your life, or you can have David Bowie to mark the stations of your life.' He smiles – black humour is never far away in his profession, he tells me later. '*Station to Station* with Bowie is better.'

Having been asked if he could contribute something to a *British Medical Journal* palliative care blog not long before, he decided to send his appraisal letter there. Popular posts on the site get around twenty replies, he says ('they'll kill me for saying that'). Soon after it was published, Taubert posted it to Twitter. The retweets began, then the Marie Curie charity joined in. A day later, Bowie's son Duncan Jones retweeted them. It was Jones's first activity on Twitter since confirming his father's death. Six months later, Jarvis Cocker read the letter out at the Royal Festival Hall. The following April, a composer, John Uren, premiered a piece setting it to music at London's Cafe Oto.

It is a moving, precious letter, completely from the heart and still online: the internet can be a place where sharing can be helpful sometimes, I say. 'Yes,' Taubert replies. 'So many people were talking about his death, though – colleagues, patients, relatives – it was a really, really big moment. But what struck me, more than anything, is that we weren't really talking about death. We were talking about living, which is the thing I actually talk about in work.'

Because we live to the very last minute of our life, Taubert goes on, the last hour of our life shouldn't be less valuable than the first hour or the middle one. Things that we think about every single day – like music, food, sex and desire – should surely hold the same worth then, too. 'All the things that might make life interesting or worth living or even miserable still apply to that moment in time. And I think it was obvious to everyone that Bowie was still really living.'

*

In late 2016, my family of three had moved out of London into the countryside of the Welsh borders. I'd fallen in love with this part of the country a decade before, going to the early Green Man festivals, watching the Black Mountains suddenly appearing on the horizon from the car, seductive in their sublimity. It was a peaceful but dramatic part of the country, its quietness only pierced by occasional planes from nearby army camps and annual gatherings of 20,000 people clamouring to hear music. Even in the biblical Powys rain of August 2010, I remember watching Joanna Newsom onstage and thinking, I need to be here, inhaling the bigger skies, filtering myself into the elements.

The romance remained, and was shared by my husband, and with a two-year-old in tow, we ran away from our busy, urban lives. But from my position in the driving seat of my new car – a necessity when your nearest neighbours are a field of sheep and a farm down a track that begins with a cattle grid – I realised nature is not always a comforter. My first autumn drives involved frightening dark mornings, my wheels turning around bends to startle deer, their eyes flashing in the gaze of my headlamps, tiny atomic bombs, their bodies becoming golden, on fire. In evenings came the fog, high-togged, with the ability to smother and kill. I remember driving home one Halloween night, and the fog lifting only once, to reveal a man dressed as the rabbit from *Donnie Darko*. I couldn't have music on in this weather. I needed to use all my senses to get home in one piece.

The next spring was the most beautiful I have ever encountered. Every colour of the landscape had its dial turned up to eleven, the skies a raspberry Panda Pop blue, the grass a Spectrum 48K acid green, the rapeseed fields startling neon-yellow, like Hacienda stripes on the hillsides. At the same time, I'd finally started emptying the dusty boxes of CDs that I'd moved from house to house for six years, and not opened since having an iPod. I found *The Colour of Spring*. It became my accompaniment to my new life, and all the new pleasures it would bring.

I'd first become interested in Talk Talk when 'It's My Life' and 'Life's What You Make It' were reissued as singles in 1990. At first I didn't know if I liked Mark Hollis's voice or not: it was reedy, high and nasal, more like an unusual instrument than something that belonged to a human being. Their videos, which I saw on *Top of the Pops*, were weird too. One had Mark Hollis in a zoo, right next to the elephants and giraffes, not singing, black dots and lines obscuring his mouth. 'It's my life,' his voice sang from somewhere in the mix. 'Don't you forget.' He was impudent. Brazen. I liked him.

I had put both songs on a mixtape which I took on package holidays with my family. Even now, these two songs take me instantly to airless living rooms in aparthotels in Tossa De Mar and the Algarve, the heat also rising from my anxiety, because I was playing a bit of myself, out loud, in front of everyone, at the height of my adolescence. I only found out years later who Mark Hollis was: a bloke with a thick London accent, born in Tottenham, whose older brother, Eddie, had managed pub rock band Eddie and the Hot Rods. Mark's first band were a garage-punk trio, The Reaction, whose first song was released on a compilation album called *Streets*, a year-end round-up of British and French DIY on the Beggars Banquet label. A different version of the song appeared on Talk Talk's first album, bearing the same name as the band.

Rare interviews of Hollis online show a man with the accent of a right Cockney geezer. His no-prisoners attitude in the videos he was in also show the influence of punk. But he preferred to listen to the music of John Coltrane and Miles Davis with Gil Evans, with sideways journeys into King Crimson and prog rock. By his band's third album, he was also obsessing about Delius and impressionist composers from the turn of the twentieth century, and getting in the best session musicians to bolster his ambitions. These included Steve Winwood of Traffic and the Spencer Davis Group on organ and Pentangle's Danny Thompson on double bass. Alongside bandmates Paul Webb and Lee Harris and collaborator Tim Friese-Greene, he started making the music he really wanted to make.

These were the tracks that came with me in the car, as my new life started to open up. I loved the first three – 'Happiness Is Easy', 'I Don't Believe in You', my old favourite 'Life's What You Make It' – conventional songs with tiny elements of weirdness scratching away in the arrangements. An isolated but twisted drum break here; a flourish of harp before frightened strings there; some shuddering, spiky harmonicas. And then there was track

four, with its whispering introductory hiss and soft flutters in stereo sound. 'Here she comes,' Mark Hollis sang,
purposefully. 'Silent in her sound.'

'April 5th' begins with quiet, synthesised percussion,
twitching, fluttering, from right speaker to left and back
again, a breath of soprano saxophone, a piano playing with
an inverted minor-key figure, rising and falling like a sigh.
Then comes the arrival of the season – 'gentle spring', all
'fresh upon the ground' – and the visual splendour of it all
as the album's title arrives in the lyrics.

Spring is female in 'April 5th'. It is giving, inviting. There
is 'laughter in her kiss' and 'shame upon her lips'. Hollis wills
her to come. The song moves delicately but with deftness,
dexterity, trying to glory in every precise moment. 'Let me
breathe,' Mark repeats at its end. I find out later that April
5th was the birthday of his wife of over thirty years, the
mother of his two sons.

'April 5th' was less a song to me that spring than an
atmosphere. It conferred a peace on this new time of my
life in which I wanted to lose myself. Its quietness, however,
made me think it was always threatening to disappear; there
was a riskiness about it even being there, and being mine. I
had to take time to stand back and observe this sound-world
in every detail to savour it, or be brave and enter it fully. It
was about stillness and space, which reflected the new place
I lived in. It felt like the right soundtrack for a stranger, yet
calmer new time in my life.

The spring of 2018 felt different but still special when
I had 'April 5th' playing along with me. It came after a
long, snowy winter: every branch, every leaf, every flower
coming alive a little later, in tiny, anxious movements. The

next spring felt different. I couldn't think of these songs without the person who had made them, whose death was announced suddenly, who hadn't made any music for years.

Talk Talk's albums after *The Colour of Spring* had been 1988's *Spirit of Eden* and 1991's *Laughing Stock*, impressionistic epics that have long been cited as career highs by both fans and critics. Seven years later, Hollis's eponymous solo album followed, plus a small sliver of piano accompaniment on a track called 'Chaos' by James Lavelle's UNKLE project. His last publicly available composition was a small one, 'Arb Section 1', originally for a film called *Peacock*, scored by the American composer Brian Reitzell, who had also brought My Bloody Valentine's Kevin Shields out of retirement. Made in 2010, it is an eerie, evocative miniature, repeating a slow, deep woodwind motif around snatches of harried, synthesised vocals, putting me in mind of contemporary artists like Oneohtrix Point Never. It ended up being used on an episode of the Kelsey Grammer TV series *Boss*, which feels like an odd ending for the Mark Hollis catalogue.

But as I was stuck in traffic one day, trying to find something to listen to on my phone, I remembered Mark had released something else. In 2013, *Natural Order* had come out, a new Talk Talk *Best of*. When I got home, I pored over my copy of *Spirit of Talk Talk*, a book by the band's illustrator James Marsh, journalist Chris Roberts and designer Toby Benjamin, and discovered that Hollis, not his label, had led the project. I later found out that a record label director I knew, Nigel Reeve, was in charge of Talk Talk's reissues. I had worked with Reeve on liner notes for a New Order box set; he was also in charge of Bowie's back catalogue. In other words, he was an authority when it came to artistic legacy.

One morning, I email Reeve nervously, asking why he thought such a private person wanted to curate another best-of collection in the years when he wanted to put Talk Talk behind him. Later that day, we speak for an hour on the phone about their friendship; it had begun in 2003 after Reeve put together an anthology of the band, *Introducing . . . Talk Talk*, which included none of the band's hits, but did feature three B-sides: a discordant, avant-garde piano version of 1983's 'Call in the Night Boy', 1986's 'It's Getting Late in the Evening' and 1988's 'John Cope'. Reeve tried to transcribe the lyrics for 'John Cope', and checked them with Hollis, who corrected them. Their relationship built from there. 'And we just started talking and talking.'

Reeve remembers a man who would meet up with him in the pub after work, always with a Guinness in his hand, where they'd talk about things that he loved. For Hollis, these included mid-century films like *The Servant*, *The Entertainer*, *A Taste of Honey* and *This Sporting Life*, the architecture of the Southbank Centre, random episodes of *The Sweeney*, and talking about how Paul McCartney's 'We All Stand Together' – also known as the Frog Chorus – was unforgivable. ('He also had a thing about the Chuckle Brothers,' Reeve later messages me. 'They gave us hours of amusement after a couple of pints.') Finding out these details made me euphoric. A man whose work was so artistically intricate, so tender, had been an ordinary human being too, a daft bugger, like so many of us.

Hollis also loved crate-digging on an extreme level for garage-rock, the music he started off making, Reeve said. 'He just loved the concept of musicians being impulsive, just as he loved jazz musicians being impulsive, which is where

Spirit of Eden came from too. As long as the one note made sense, that was all that mattered to Mark.'

That logic extended to him assembling a new Talk Talk retrospective, which showed his intentions for where he'd wanted his sonic ambitions to go. It begins with 'Have You Heard the News?' from their debut, which takes a mood that's a relative of early Tears for Fears records but more peculiar and intimate. It ends with 'Taphead' from *Laughing Stock*, seven minutes and twenty-six seconds of slow, languorous outlandishness. 'He just wanted something that literally sounded like the natural order of things.'

Hollis and Reeve worked together with more than twenty sequences of the final ten tracks. Mark spent weeks tinkering with their arrangement, including altering the milliseconds between each track – and then the album 'kind of quietly came out, and got reviews, but there was no great marketing for it. He wanted none of that noise.' And with that, Hollis was done and went back to the things he loved: travelling the length of Chile on an off-road motorcycle with a friend, enjoying train journeys across dramatic landscapes. I feel so excited to hear all this, I say to Reeve, because I want to know more things about the people whose music has soundtracked my life – although it feels wrong saying that too, because I respect his desire to peel away from people he didn't know, and to get on with his own existence.

Reeve pauses to reflect, and then speaks again, his voice full of warmth. 'Mark was intensely intelligent, very funny, and the most normal person you could ever meet. But I think the key to his music is [that], because so few people knew him well . . . their only touchpoint with him was the music. That was their way into Mark and the way out of

Mark. There was nothing else but those sounds. And that was what he would have wanted.'

Perhaps we grieve musicians we never met because we imagine these are people we would like, people we want to be with, because we connect strongly with their songs. We often feel like we are hearing the ultimate expression of their souls, which, of course, sometimes we're not – sometimes we are only hearing the parts they want to articulate loudly and want us to hear.

But sometimes these musicians have spent years crafting their music so it is absolutely what they wanted, so when we hear them, we are hearing people channelling their creativity at us directly. They are never bored or tired of us as listeners either. Their songs are conversations we complete as encouraging friends. Part of who we are also makes these people whole, makes them ours, as we fill in the spaces in their songs with elements of our very different lives.

When we listen to a musician we love after they are gone, that experience gains another undeniable dimension. When a track or album of theirs comes to an end, we know its maker is no longer out there somewhere, about to make more music – and so we may mourn that our ability to carry on those conversations with them has been lost. But we can always spend more time with what they have left us already: new dimensions of the work will open up and let us enter them as we grow older and change. The spark first lit when we loved them doesn't have to be pined for: it hasn't gone out. We can hear their voice whispered into our willing ear as if it was for the first time because we are still listening.

Track 11

Pressure Drop – Toots and The Maytals

Why Music Is Still There at the End

On a September morning in 2018, a few months after I'd turned forty, I sat in the Octagon Room of the Orleans House Gallery in Twickenham, a few metres away from the shiny, silver ribbon of the Thames. I took in the ceiling of pale blue, white and gold, Georgian cherubs lounging over the fireplace, windows looking out to late-summer grass and ripe trees, the shiny black-and-white chequerboard floor, the Alice in Wonderland playfulness of it all.

Around me were familiar faces in bright colours, creating rows of tight rainbows. Our friend Pat had died three weeks earlier. He was only forty-one. I looked at Kat, his beloved wife, my good friend, in her red stiletto boots, and I thought of my mother in a crematorium in Swansea nearly thirty-five years earlier. I wondered how she had felt in that moment, how she had processed that experience, if the hymns she had chosen for the day gave her a moment to reflect, or to feel something that wasn't distress or detachment.

Dad's ashes were buried in the crematorium grounds. Kat had scattered Pat's ashes downstream in Richmond-on-Thames, at his request, where they'd gone on an early date together. We were all standing behind her, in the same place that Pat and Kat married, listening to the last of the three songs he had written down for us all to hear.

It began with a signature flourish of classic reggae: a drum fill beginning with a high-tuned, crisp snare, propelling itself forward to three ringing hits of the tom. Then came the song's joyful foundations: a lean, sprightly bassline laying out a major triad arpeggio, the ringing keys of a piano, stuttering guitars. And then the voices came in, humming a melody blissfully, almost serenely, but with a little flicker of swagger. To me, Toots Hibbert's voice has always sounded carefree but knowing, relaxed yet also conscious of the weight of the world.

'Pressure Drop' marked the end of the memorial to a man so many people had loved. As it played, we felt our limbs stir, our feet twitch, something in the air lift for three minutes. As it faded, I realised that a song's emotional effects are never subject to a sudden, clunky, cassette-player stop. And every time I've heard 'Pressure Drop' since, I've thought about the people in that room, how we are unusual custodians of the song now, carrying it in an altered, heightened way through our ordinary days, our longer lives.

*

In 2012, Tia DeNora, Professor of Sociology of Music at the University of Exeter, wrote a paper called 'Resounding the Great Divide: Theorising music in everyday life at the end of life'. She discussed how music can be used not only in end-of-life situations, but as 'one type of cultural material that can be used . . . for the figuring of narratives . . . about those times'.

DeNora discusses a case involving the music of the violinist Andre Rieu, and how it affected a family. One family member, whom DeNora calls S, is a former dancer dying of a degenerative disease who has just discovered his music. She shares it with her daughter one day. It bonds them together. They talk about how music makes you want to dance to it and S's daughter squeezes her mother's feet, moving them in time.

Eighteen months after the mother's death, the daughter is at home sitting with her father, J, when she chances upon a classical concert while channel-hopping. J is now bed-bound and gravely ill, but has had a happy day, having been visited by friends and family. He thinks the music he is hearing is beautiful; his daughter looks to see who is playing, and it's Andre Rieu. She lets him enjoy the music alone for a moment, then talks about her experience with her mother.

'The daughter again feels a surge of emotion; J recognises this; they have "reconnected" with S. They reminisce about S,' DeNora writes. 'Music that was already significant in the family culture acquires an additional layer of meaning . . . the music "holds" the experience of connection to S . . . and therefore between all three.' S seemed 'vividly present' in that musical moment, the family said: the fact that it linked to her love of music as something to dance to made it feel like the song was embodying her.

Thinking about the concept of a musical 'afterlife' sheds new light on how to remember an individual's identity and presence. 'Pressure Drop' affected me on that September day because I knew Pat was a huge music-lover. I was at the memorial as a close friend of Kat's, but I'd first met him years before I knew her, at a Sunday afternoon folk and blues club he ran near King's Cross in London, called In The Pines. I also knew of his fabulous dancing from Track And Field and the garage-dominated Frat Shack; he was an insanely cool dresser, in impeccable Mod glasses and sharp jackets.

He was also a brilliant music writer at *Select* and the *NME* before he moved up the latter's editorial ranks – ultimately he became Head of News Development at *The Times* – but he was also gentle and funny, entirely without ego. Often covering acts that were slightly wayward, like Broadcast, The Horrors and Dungen, he also wrote a great history of the *NME* pulling sensitive, revelatory details from writers like Danny Baker and Paul Morley. The tweets when he died spoke of his coolness and kindness. 'He was the only one of us who could have been on the cover,' said Dorian Lynskey, an old colleague. 'A lovely man and a fine writer.'

I never knew Pat loved reggae, but I guessed this song must have meant something to him, or that it was chosen to convey something. But it was an unusual, surprising choice for a wake – and I wondered if this was also part of his generosity, as well as his charm.

'Pressure Drop' was also a song that was always around on the radio, the TV, part of the fabric of everyday existence. DeNora speculated that the 'musical happenstance' of the father and daughter happening upon Andre Rieu on TV gave them comfort 'that [the mother's] spirit would live on in various ways and sometimes through serendipitous practices as a part of daily life'. She added: 'These practices in turn underline music's role as a quasi-sacred medium for everyday spirituality . . . music offers yet another means with which to reach across the "great" divide.' I wondered if picking a well-known song would have meant the same to Pat, even if the idea to do so was only unconsciously rippling through.

*

In summer 2021, I ask Kat if she would mind talking to me about the song. I approach her tentatively. She enthusiastically says yes. We meet in a tapas bar on The Cut in London's Waterloo which we have both known and loved for years: its place in our separate pasts is a comfort, and we laugh at how little there has changed. As we chat, and I watch the Dictaphone's clock tick on second by second, I try to be a good friend above anything else, around the patatas bravas, the padron peppers, the large glasses of lunchtime white wine.

Pat and Kat had been together since 2009; they found out about his tumour one morning after he had collapsed on the floor the night before. Thirty per cent of the tumour was inoperable, liable to grow and mutate. Pat and Kat married. They did their jobs, went on holidays. Two years after that, Pat typed up his funeral wishes. Three years later, his sister read some words from it at the memorial. 'You shouldn't be sad. I'm off to join the universe and I'm excited,' it said.

On the other side of the paper, three songs were listed. One was the Adagio from Bach's Violin Concerto no. 2 in E Major. Another was 'Nut Rocker', a 1962 number one by B. Bumble and the Stingers. This turns Tchaikovsky's theme from *The Nutcracker* into a jangly, piano-propelled giddy rush of novelty. Often used as shorthand for pep and cheek on film or TV, it also flagged up Pat's love of daft rock and roll records. 'Typical, typical Pat,' Kat says, laughing. Do you think he put it there to wind you up? 'Of course he did, Jude. Of course he did!'

Kat and I talk about how the funeral songs we often hear today are different to those we heard when we were younger, how we now live in a more secular society that has more emphasis on the individual than the ritual. Nevertheless, sensitivity and delicacy are still required when picking the right songs; naturally, we have to consider the people who will be hearing them. Kat couldn't bring herself to play 'Nut Rocker'. 'Imagine!' Nor did she want to play 'just sad classical music' at the memorial. 'It wouldn't seem right just to do that. You still want to celebrate the essence of that person, don't you? You want to bottle a little bit of them somehow.'

'Pressure Drop' was the third song on Pat's list. 'Pressure Drop' felt different. Kat sat down to listen to it with Pat's mother and sister after his death, and they knew instantly that it felt right. 'A lot of the lyrics are heavy, but there's a momentum and lightness there. And it was important to have that mood in the room on that day . . . that felt right to me, and that all came from him.'

We talk about what happened after we heard it: we went to a pub just downriver for the wake, old friends chatting and remembering Pat, reconnecting the old bonds we had with each other, as songs played through the garden. Kat is beaming. 'The whole day was filled with music, wasn't it? It was the best way we could represent him. Not rows of people wearing black, queueing up to say he was lovely, then going off to the buffet.'

She'd hoped 'Pressure Drop' would give everyone a boost, but she hadn't reckoned on its long-term effects. After the ceremony, lots of people contacted her about the song, which was something she didn't expect. 'I guess people will remember a song more easily than they'll remember a paragraph from a eulogy,' she says, thoughtfully. 'And good songs hover and linger . . . and what matters is that it's a song that acts on people straightaway – there's an immediacy in it where you're instantly transported. We will look for things in songs because that's what we need at that time, won't we? That's what makes music something we come back to again and again in any era of our lives.'

*

Just over two years after Pat died, Toots Hibbert followed him in September 2020. What friends they would have been in my fantastical daydreams: bumping into each other at a celestial bar, cherubs recumbent above them, Pat in an impeccable mac, nursing a pint and adjusting his specs, Toots in his regular leather waistcoat and gold chains, ordering the rum that fuelled his recording sessions back home in Jamaica, the two of them laughing like drains, then talking quietly, intensely, firm friends for ever.

A few weeks before he died at seventy-seven, Toots spoke to my beloved Miranda Sawyer about his first album in ten years, *Got to Be Tough*. His songwriting, he said, had always been steeped in positivity. 'In my songs, I tell a story that kids in Europe, Jamaica, America could learn something about. Every song does a lot to the audience. I make sure all my songs are positive and give confidence, elevate people, black or white.'

Toots was born in 1942, the youngest of fourteen, to a mother who died when he was eight, and a father who died three years later. In his teens, he moved to Kingston and got a job at a barbershop where he'd sing gospel songs as he cut his customers' hair. When he was eighteen, Jamaica gained independence from the UK, and vast swathes of its population migrated from the countryside to the island's cities. New music flourished from this influx of new people: ska, rock steady, and the genre that Toots would name, with a slightly different spelling, on his and The Maytals' 1968 hit, 'Do the Reggay'.

In Jason Fine's *Rolling Stone* profile of Hibbert, published less than a month before he died, Toots talked about being excited about his new music. He was a funny, free-spirited character: nowhere to be found when Fine turned up at his house, as planned, after a flight from the US; keeping peculiar hours, changing his mind breezily when he fancied it. He nevertheless enjoyed reflecting on his youth, when The Maytals were a close-harmony trio, and when Coxsone Dodd, head of the Studio One label, turned Hibbert away at an audition because his voice was 'too strange'. Toots kept coming back, and when Dodd asked him if he had any songs he brought 'Hello Honey', which became one of his first hits.

Back then, people said Hibbert's voice fluttered like a country and western instrument, but it also picked up American soul from long-wave radio. To me, it's always been as warm and as powerful as the voice of Otis Redding, transported from Georgia across the Gulf of Mexico to the deep blues of the Caribbean.

'Pressure Drop' specifically, Toots told the *Guardian*'s Dave Simpson in 2016, just 'came to him' on the guitar. Its lyric spoke of revenge but in the form of karma: 'The title was a phrase I used to say. If someone done me wrong, rather than fight them like a warrior, I'd say: "The pressure's going to drop on you."' It was a piece of advice: to be good, to know that you'll feel the pressure upon you if you diso- bey. A *Guardian* column a few days after Hibbert's death, by Kenan Malik, summed up beautifully how 'Pressure Drop' fused disparate elements: 'That was the way with

Hibbert — the melding of the blissful and the rough, the soothing and the sharp.'

I wondered what Toots would have thought about someone choosing one of his songs for their memorial. I imagined him becoming used to the praise, saying gracious thank-yous but brushing things off, letting compliments fall from his shoulders. Perhaps he no longer thought about the magnitude of a studio session becoming unplugged from a room and turning into a staple of pop culture, flying away into the muggy caverns of house parties, the dry air of radio-accompanied factory floors, the heavy atmospheres of funerals. Perhaps he even felt sadness when he reflected on those situations, when the origins of your bonds with your band become ghosts in the grooves of a record, flecks of dust on fragile reels of sepia tape, overlooked elements of a soundfile. I felt sad that I'd never be able to ask him what that was like.

And then I remembered the other Maytals who are still with us, men that played on that original song, including bassist Jackie Jackson and drummer Paul Douglas. I found their agent's email online, and a few weeks later, a WhatsApp circle was flashing on my phone, a serene, smiling face with sunglasses and a baseball cap inside it: the youthful face of the man who began the song over half a century ago, with a high-tuned, crisp snare and three ringing hits of the tom.

*

Paul Douglas is seventy-one when we speak, and living in Florida, north of Miami. It has been a tough week. Jackie

Jackson's wife died on 11 September, the anniversary of Toots' death. It has been hard on them all: the old band remain close, he tells me, talking slowly and quietly.

I ask if another time would be better. He interjects quickly, saying no – he really wanted to speak about 'Pardy'. Instead of calling someone a friend in Jamaica, he explains, 'you call them a "pardy" like a partner – he'd called me "Pardy Paul" for so many years. He'd call me at one o'clock in the night, and I'd see my phone ringing, and I'd know it was Toots. Just to say hi, for nothing. "I haven't talked to you for a little while, Pardy Paul." "Pardy, but it's [only] been a few days!" And he'd start laughing. But he was just like that. This caring person, caring for everybody.'

I talk to Paul about his musical family, and about the sixties in Jamaica after independence; how badly Rastafarians were treated, how music provided escape and empowerment in the tornado of change. He joined The Maytals in 1969 when he was only nineteen. 'My rookie years,' he adds, a sparkle of joy in his voice. They recorded 'Pressure Drop' soon after.

What details does he remember of recording it? I know it's more than half a century, I say. 'Ahhhhh . . . I don't know.' I let Paul take his time on the phone.

After a minute, his voice comes, soft and clear. 'Happiness. To be playing with Coxsone and Winston Wright and Jackie Jackson in general, all these people I looked up to – it was awesome. They never treated me differently.' He didn't realise what he was 'getting into in some ways', he goes on. 'I was just a kid having fun – but with "Pressure Drop", I just felt like this was going to be something, that this was going to have an impact, especially when Pardy started singing.'

And then he starts to hum down the line: that opening melody, soft, lilting and warm, sounding so much like the voice of his friend. I find myself welling up. 'Yeahhhhh,' Douglas sings, finishing the song's opening phrase, then he addresses his late friend in the present tense, as if he hadn't died. 'There's no one like that man. What he does and how he does his thing.'

Paul has thought about the lyric lots over the years. It was partly about the way Toots had been exploited in Jamaica's music industry, by people who were dishonest with him. 'You know how it is in the record business. And I understood what he meant.' But the song was bigger than that too. 'He also knew that problems were everywhere, so the song was international – [it] would relate to people from all walks of life. And it sounds simple . . . but if you really concentrate on what he's saying, you recognise how powerful the message is. Just be honest. There's no need for injustice. That's why it gravitated to so many people.'

Toots got on with everyone. He'd talk to people he'd just met like they were long-time friends. At gigs, he'd jump down from the stage, even in his seventies, and go to the platform where fans were sitting in wheelchairs to go and say hi. Paul 'would love to see it'.

Then I talk to him about Pat, and the memorial, and the effect the song had on us, carrying us out of the room, into the day, into the rest of our lives. I can hear the emotion in his voice as he responds, how genuinely touched he sounds. 'I feel honoured,' he says. 'Honoured that something I participated in means so much to someone else, because at the time when you're doing these things, it's just having fun.'

Before he goes, he adds, 'Please pass on my sympathies to the lady. I'm so sorry.'

I send Kat the recording of Paul singing Pat's song, and think of that hum heading into the universe, meeting him there.

*

Later that night, I think about something else Paul said to me: how he was as passionate about playing today as he was when he was a teenager. He still performs, as did Toots, in his seventies – a decade that used to be kept clear for kicking back, and a slow glide into retirement.

But many musicians of this age and older still record, even when they don't have to do so for reasons of financial need. When Paul McCartney released his eighteenth solo album in December 2020, at the age of seventy-eight-and-a-half, the question I wanted to ask him, more than anything, was this: what keeps you doing this? You could have laid back on your rock star chaise longue years ago, but you didn't. Even discounting your time with The Beatles, you wrote 'Pipes of Peace', 'Little Willow' and 'Jenny Wren', oratorios and ballet scores, made experimental ambient pieces and collaborated with Youth, the Freelance Hellraiser, Rihanna and Kanye West. You've also barely stopped touring.

McCartney's autobiography when it came wasn't even a conventional one: it told his story through songs, via conversations with the Irish poet Paul Muldoon. He tried to blame this approach on practical reasons, when the book was announced: 'The time has never been right. I know that some people, when they get to a certain age, like to go to a diary to recall day-to-day events from the past, but I have no such notebooks. What I do have are my songs, hundreds of them, which I've learned serve much the same purpose.' The thing he'd always managed to do, wherever he was, he said, was 'to write new songs'. This was what he did; these were the things that made sense of his existence, that gave him meaning and structure – as they did, of course, for so many others.

I wonder if the desire to keep writing songs or making music as artists get older is about a biological urge to keep their brains functioning in profound, instructive ways. Nina Kraus at Northwestern University in Evanston, Illinois, runs an auditory neuroscience lab called Brainvolts that investigates sound processing in the brain. Her team has researched how playing a musical instrument changes how older adults relate to the world, which helps them become more involved in everyday interactions. This works both in terms of what they can observe and understand as people, but also how they can communicate.

I speak to Kraus on the phone one day and revel in her enthusiasm. Even if you've played an instrument many years before, she tells me, that has an impact on your older brain. 'If you have a musical experience in the past . . . just for a couple of years, that has a legacy. These people have better, crisper sound processing in these areas that ordinarily become diminished by ageing . . . and I see this first-hand looking at neurons, looking at cells that change.'

These neurons will even change their response to sound well into old age. 'So sound connects us with the world . . . the hearing brain is vast. It engages.' It helps, Kraus adds, taking me back to the beginning of my explorations, that music 'is very, very linked with memory'. Here I think of McCartney telling his story through his songs, and me telling mine. 'And if you think about our sense of self and who we are, you know, we really are our memories and our experiences. There is such a strong link between memory and who we are – and music and who we are.'

Then Kraus describes music as a portal, and at last I realise it's the best term to describe its effects. It is a grand, exhilarating entrance to something. It is a way of accessing new, exciting sensory information. A portal is also a biological term, which provides a fittingly visceral analogy: it is part of an organism through which things enter and exit us, before leaving behind powerful, lingering effects.

A portal also allows us a way into people, Kraus argues, when other means of communication become limited. 'Music is a portal into the brain of a person who has difficulty remembering where they fit in to the world.'

*

When I moved back to Wales as an adult to be nearer my family, I made a new dear friend, Jess George. She connected me to my musical past, because we'd been at the opposite edges of the same, sprawling friendship group as teenagers, even though we went to different schools. We'd go to the same gigs and dance at the same clubs: we were even in the same gang at the cinema to watch *Trainspotting* in the summer of 1996, where I'd first heard Iggy Pop's 'Lust for Life' and Brian Eno's 'Deep Blue Day'. In our late thirties we made up for never managing to get to know each other properly before, bonding over psychedelia, funk, eerie folk, Northern Soul and big pop, feeling the semiquavers, quavers and crotchets act like magnets for two old Swansea girls.

Jess had left home to study occupational therapy at university, qualifying in 1999; she has worked in older adult mental health and dementia care since 2007. Her profession is driven by how 'occupations' build meaning in our life, occupations being the activities we need and want to do, to bond us to people we need to be with, and our environments. 'And as far back as my first job – with people that were experiencing mild memory and cognitive problems, to people who were in more severe stages – I noticed that at every point, music meant something to people. It was always the thing that made lights come on in their eyes.'

Practically, Jess explains to me over a Saturday night takeaway curry in my living room, she found this out in different ways. She played CDs from the years of people's childhoods to spark reminiscences and talked about songs that they might have sung at school or church, or that their parents might have sung to them. She spent a lot of time singing 'Wind the Bobbin Up', a song closely connected to the cotton mill industry, in the early days of her career in northern England. 'The way we could sing a song together showed the other person feelings of trust and love,' she says. 'You could have that kind of love for each other without having to say it.'

Jess learned more about dementia in her practice and postgraduate study as her career progressed; she underlines to me that dementia is an umbrella term for different progressive disorders affecting the brain. She also discovered how language is often lost quickly, but that music processing is usually retained. She then recalls 'a gentleman', she says, tenderly, that she worked with some years ago. He had been a successful professional musician, and she worked with him when his dementia was at a later stage.

At one point, he was in hospital and unable to verbally communicate, experiencing 'extreme distress'. One day, an old friend phoned the ward and asked if there was anything he could do to help. Jess asked him to recommend some songs she could play, 'but he actually did something much better than that'. Soon after, four CDs arrived in the post from the caller, all of them playlists for different phases of his friend's life. 'I'll never forget when I put on the CD, and the first track by B. B. King started – and he froze. Although it was more than that: it was like some sort of heavenly possession.'

Jess isn't religious at all, she points out. 'But it was this profound reaction. It's like a face suddenly seeing light. I've seen it many times before. It's almost like the person has heard the voice of God.' And then came a miracle. 'At this stage, he couldn't form a full sentence, but then, out of nowhere he went: "I can see my room, my teenage room."' He described it to Jess in clear phrases and zoomed in on a few details; she laughs as she remembers a 'saucy poster, on his wall'. 'I was watching someone being transported. And not only was he there, in the past, but he could actually find the words to take me there too.'

Jess has also supported people with dementia to attend dance groups. She recalls one person who could no longer live on her own, wash or dress, teaching Jess how to line dance, as soon as the music started. She also took a married couple, where the husband had been his wife's carer for years, to another session. 'And he said he saw his wife for an hour like the person she used to be, that the music seemed to bring her alive.'

Music brings up other parts of people that are repressed, like their sexuality, Jess adds – 'because it's good to remember that not all sexuality is about having sex. It's about connecting with your own identity, your sociability – and it's also about remembering who you were through other parts of your life.' I ask whether her work has made her feel more profoundly about her own attachment to music, and suddenly we're off discussing our own stories. Jess grins broadly at one memory: she's a small child dancing on the shiny wooden floor in the front room of her old terraced house in Port Tennant in Swansea, to her first record, an ABBA album that she'd asked her parents to buy her.

'I suppose there comes a point in your life when you realise, this is my music,' she says later, talking about how music assisted her transition from childhood to adulthood. 'You don't know whether it's the music or whether it's you, but suddenly you feel like a new you. To me, music was almost always a soundtrack to the new. It made me understand things in new ways. When I'm thinking about what we love in our lives, about all those human experiences, what we all have through it all is music, to the end. It stays there for almost all of us.'

*

In his bestselling 2008 book *Musicophilia*, neurologist Oliver Sacks presents his case for how music occupies more areas of the brain than language. He does so by talking about patients he had known professionally, and about the incredible framework that had bound them all together.

There is no human culture in which [music] is not highly developed and esteemed. Its very ubiquity may cause it to be trivialised in daily life: we may switch on a radio, switch it off, hum a tune, tap our feet, find the words of an old song going through our minds, and think nothing of it. But to those who are lost in dementia, the situation is different. Music is no luxury to them, but a necessity, and can have a power to restore them to themselves, and to others, at least for a while.

I think about other people who have died far too young – about my father, about Pat – and about how essential music was to them too, how their songs have outlived them, but lived on in other people's lives. I think about myself getting older, and how music is still something I reach for and yearn for. I think about how it might shape me in the years that come next, the new friendships that might be fostered through songs, the new associations they may spark, the new stories waiting to be written. Music is no luxury to any of us. It is a necessity that helps all of us restore ourselves to ourselves.

Track 12

I Trawl the Megahertz –
Prefab Sprout

When Music Comes Out of the Silence

I was driving on the high, snaking slopes of the Graig, the dark-green-crested hill overlooking the village that had now been my home for four years, when the song came out of the speakers. This was a new route for me – single-track, pitted, perilous, overwhelming. It was late April, a few days before my forty-second birthday. That spring had been fantastical, phosphorescent, frightening, unreal.

It had also been quiet. No cars. No people. For the last month, our family of three had looped each other around the house like stunned spiders, tightening our web, trying to make sense of this new sphere of silence.

The year had come to life for me three months before, not on the first of January, or even on the eleventh, an anniversary I am able to cope with much more easily these days, but the tenth. The tenth was important to me that year because of my son. On this date, he would be five years, eight months and twelve days old, the exact age I had been when Dad died.

I had not needed a calculator to plot out this milestone. My son had been born a day before my birthday, and one day I thought about how sweet it was that he was seeing every season at the same stage in life that I did in mine. I had thought about my dad a lot when my little boy had turned five, but around Christmas, this upcoming way-marker suddenly appeared with frightening clarity. My son was about to reach the age I was when I had been asked a question at the doorstep. I wanted to soak up every bit of him in those hours, be there with him with every atom of my being. But I wanted to make the tenth of January an ordinary day too, not freighted with drama.

That day, the weather was brighter than it usually was for early January. It was also a Friday, a school day, and as I waited to get my son off on the school bus, I thought about the cuddle I would give him. He had also known about the existence of my father for a few weeks by this point, after finding a photograph of the two of us on my desk in my office. I kicked myself when he saw it. He asked me who it was. I explained that I had another daddy when I was little, who had been poorly and died, but now he was in me and Uncle Jon, and we loved him very much. I had had two daddies, I added, and I had a little brother, Uncle James, which made me very lucky.

My son asked lots of questions while looking at the photo, full of blunt, beautiful curiosity. Was he nice? What food did he like? What is a moustache? I answered them simply, with a smile, and got out some pizzas for our end-of-the-week tea. I then put on a playlist I had made and felt very conscious about doing so, about the songs that I wanted to pass on to him; I didn't want to impose myself too much. Still, I loved that he now sang along to Wham!'s 'Freedom', and always laughed as I tried to hit George's high note at the end of the chorus, and always spectacularly failed. He would shout 'ooh-baby-baby' along to Salt 'N' Pepa's 'Push It' (I always sang loudly over the line about them 'getting pissed'). His brief interest in the Pet Shop Boys' 'Paninaro', sadly, had waned, but Saint Etienne's 'Nothing Can Stop Us' still had him jiggling. 'This lady sounds nice,' he had said when he was three. I was pleased to report back – from many interviews, after loving many Saint Etienne albums – that Sarah Cracknell certainly was.

In the three weeks that followed that day, I finished the proposal for the book you now hold in your hand, but outside our little bubble, other things were happening in the world. On 10 January, Public Health England published its first short statement about a new disease that had been detected in a city in China. Three months later, nearly a thousand people were dying in the UK every day, and I was leaving my house twice a week to get milk, a five-minute drive down long rural lanes, turning to parallel the peaks of the Skirrid and the Sugarloaf to the south-west, the volume in the car turned up high, as I tried to find music to soothe me. *The Colour of Spring* wasn't working its magic this year. In those unfamiliar early days of the first Covid lockdown, disappearing into familiar albums felt uncomfortably dissonant, each note belonging to a very different me, and a very different world.

I didn't know why this was happening. I was still writing about music for work, but the process felt strangely dislocated. I was able to convey my passion in words – I did a primer on the work of PJ Harvey for the *Guardian*, full of love – but not properly feel the emotions as I listened to the songs. I panicked. Music had always been my medicine, but now it wasn't, and – oh God – my future plans involved writing a book about how much it could move us.

But I wasn't the only one who couldn't feel its effects at certain points in the pandemic. Daniel Dylan Wray wrote a column for The Quietus later that year about how music for him had similarly ceased to become 'an anchor on command'.

Some albums, no matter if serene or batshit intense, felt like trying to force down a mountainous Sunday dinner after forty-eight hours on the whizz. It felt like music stopped working for me, as though the part of my brain that usually leapt to attention upon its arrival was wading and slowly sinking in tar. The one thing in my life always capable of cutting through the noise and mayhem of the world and delivering me to another place altogether, was all of a sudden adding to the noise.

I knew there were some people, of course, who didn't feel pleasure when they listened to music at all, even outside international health crises – I used to refer to them jokingly as Tory culture ministers. But then I found out that roughly 5 per cent of people have musical anhedonia, a condition first given a name in 2011. Anhedonia usually involves a failure to experience pleasure from stimuli that a person once enjoyed, but musical anhedonia is either the result of a death of tissue after injury, or it is built into the structure of a person's brain from their birth.

In those who have it, there are very few neurological connections between the part of the brain that perceives and processes information from sound and the dopamine-drizzled reward pathways that I have written about before. But then I thought: if 5 per cent of people have this, that means 95 per cent of people don't. In other words, the vast majority of human beings feel music moving them, and many of those won't even be rabid music fans.

So, what had happened to me? The pandemic had engendered isolation, which had severed our real-world, physical connections. Music had become something we mainly accessed using the same screens that were delivering horror to us second by second in a rolling live feed. 'An underactive reward system dampens an individual's motivation to engage in activities that are usually experienced as pleasurable,' wrote Sarah L. Hegarty of Stanford University in her May 2020 paper 'The Impact of COVID-19 on Mental Health: The interactive roles of brain biotypes and human connection'. '[Our] efforts are not reinforced with a requisite sense of reward, including anticipatory reward. In the context of this dysfunctional reinforcement cycle, sources of stimulation become increasingly limited and the anhedonia worsens.'

Our scope for spontaneous encounters was vastly reduced as were opportunities for new sources of stimulation and joy. Wray's piece underlined how music is not just about the ears either when it's experienced away from home. 'It is a multi-sensory experience,' he wrote, 'from the sweat and pulse of a club to the stench of stagnant gig venue carpets . . . from rifling through fusty charity shop records to perfectly programmed light shows that dazzle the eye.' He learned to get back into music by readjusting his expectations of himself, by not forcing himself to gorge on new music and culture, because '[that's] what I normally do and is expected of me'. Instead, he let himself embrace 'the disconnect, and subsequent void, allowed a gentle reset to take place' and gradually let his 'natural curiosity and . . . insatiable hunger' return.

Thankfully, I had managed to do the same. I admit it: sometimes music can be too much. Sometimes the amount of it when you're a critic – as well as the meaning of it when you're a music-lover – can overwhelm. A month into the pandemic, I threw off my critic's beret and tried to get back to basics. I made indulgent, stream-of-consciousness playlists for my moods, and interviewed artists who were doing the same. I found comfort in generous voices on the radio and let them do my musical discovery for me. I also let myself get obsessed with specific older songs.

By mid-April, I had one that seemed to be working for me on my twice-weekly drives to get a four-pint bottle of milk from a safe, outdoor fridge. This was 'The Night' by Frankie Valli & the Four Seasons. I loved wailing along to it in the car – singing the bassline, the organ line, tchhh-ing along to the fizz of the tambourine, ba-ba-ing the second verse brass, grunting along to the orchestral glissando and crescendo in the middle-eight, which felt like a scratchy, sped-up approximation of the similar moment in The Beatles' 'A Day in the Life'. I realised later I was drawn to 'The Night' because it had been a highlight of my joint 40th birthday party disco with Jess just over two years ago, played by my dear friend Ian, with whom I used to DJ in London and run a blog about our love of band T-shirts, and that I had danced to it with other people from school, tertiary college, university, old workplaces and different corners of parenthood and adulthood. I realised I'd missed these people so much. Playing the song took me to them.

But on that late April morning, as the track finished again, I decided to take a longer, windier route home for a change, and another track started, one I hadn't heard for a few years. I had accidentally enabled the Spotify radio algorithm, which usually worked terribly, but today proved the theory of exceptions to rules. It began with a long, looping string melody, one that swooped down in pitch, that didn't fit into a regular rhythm, that felt unshackled somehow, out of time.

I knew what the track was straightaway – and I knew it was twenty-two minutes long, and that I wanted to hear it all, now. I felt myself driving around lanes I didn't know to it, getting lost in it, regaining my sense of direction in it, as I let it play out into the hills.

Its first line was delivered by a woman with a deep, expressionless American accent, and she was speaking not singing. She said: 'I am telling myself the story of my life.'

*

I first heard 'I Trawl the Megahertz', the title track of the album of the same name, in the summer of 2004. Back then, I was living with my friend Kathryn, a huge fount of knowledge about obscure indiepop, female-fronted rap, foreign-language records and Bucks Fizz. We lived in a flat in Lower Clapton, East London, which smelled of the fried chicken shop downstairs and a green tea-fragranced air freshener stuck optimistically but hopelessly in the hall, and we got to it via a rusty, gridded gate and a long pitted pathway. The track came through the walls from Kathryn's room one night, and she told me it was by Paddy McAloon: to me, the curtain-haired, floppy-fringed frontman of Prefab Sprout who sang about hot dogs and jumping frogs. When I think of him even now, I'm still instantly reminded of the record shelves just past the tills in Gateways supermarket in Gorseinon in 1988, and a little girl savouring the surreal, carefree poetry of the chorus of 'The King of Rock and Roll'.

I listened to 'I Trawl the Megahertz' lying back on the bed, being introduced to a woman with flint eyes in a kerosene dress spending twelve days in Paris waiting for her life to start. She sounded like a glamorous character, her voice deep and flat like a solid, glistening line. She told us that she was setting out her stall behind a sheet of dark hair.

All of the summer was hers. She was not living in any realm I understood and I liked that. I wanted to be her, even for a moment, even though she was 'living in a lullaby'.

I remember reading Paddy McAloon's liner notes in the booklet. He started writing the album after two bouts of eye surgery when he wasn't able to read or use a computer. He passed the time listening to radio programmes, and bought himself a scanner, recording snatches of audio, including material from phone-ins and chat shows and encrypted military conversations. I read the liner notes again, seventeen years later. 'It seems to be a portrait of a woman who is trying to make sense of her life by reviewing selected memories,' Paddy begins. I love that 'seems' – as if her character is a visitation.

'She is like someone with their hand on a radio dial, tuning into distant stations, listening to fragments of different broadcasts,' he continues. Then he had started editing what he had heard in his head. Short passages from documentaries would 'cross-pollinate with melancholy confidences aired on late night phone-ins'; phrases that 'originated in different time zones on different frequencies would team up to make new and oddly affecting sentences'.

In spring 2020, the words that hit me in the car felt concrete and clean. I heard myself in all of her words. I heard a woman describing a life that began with joyful mysteries, and how she was trying to capture things that remained elusive. She was talking of receivers 'that may help us make sense of who we are and where we came from'. At one point she was 'tying a shoelace' when a 'comet thrills the sky' – the stellar equivalent of me, when I was little, listening to Wham! in the school changing room.

I felt like she was talking to me. I was trying to work out who I was through the songs I had loved in my life, and trying to work out what kind of role I was performing in this whole pattern – but what was I doing? The narrator told me. 'Ever the dull alchemist, I have before me together all the necessary elements. It is their combination that eludes me.'

'I Trawl the Megahertz' also made me worry about what I was planning to do with my book. 'Anything that doesn't fit my narrow interpretation/ I will carelessly discard,' the woman said – and I worried that I might not be telling the best story, or the right story. It's a fact that this book could have featured a completely different set of songs. Somehow, there aren't chapters on Bronski Beat's 'Smalltown Boy', New Order's 'True Faith', Desireless's 'Voyage Voyage', Madonna's 'Like a Prayer', Electronic's 'Getting Away With It', New Kids On The Block's 'I'll Be Loving You Forever', Jon Secada's 'Just Another Day', Ride's 'Vapour Trail', Kirsty MacColl's 'In These Shoes', Will Young's 'Leave Right Now', Burial's 'Distant Lights', Hot Chip's 'Flutes', John Grant's 'Pale Green Ghosts', Lisa Knapp's 'Searching for Lambs', Lankum's 'The Wild Rover', Keeley Forsyth's 'Start Again', Ed Dowie's 'The Obvious I', Self Esteem's 'I Do This All the Time'.

'Riding through Wagnerian opera, you learn some, if not all, of the language,' the Megahertz woman says, taunting me. 'And these are the footsteps you follow, the tracks of impossible love.'

The woman also talked about someone distant, more mysterious, who lingered in her life. She felt a 'longing for bliss in the arms of some beloved from the past'. Her eyes were still 'often fixed upon/ The place I last saw you.' And then she quoted some lines McAloon had clearly discovered on a phone-in or a talk show, from a woman going through a divorce, which gained a different meaning in my discombobulated mind. 'I said "Your daddy loves you" / I said "Your daddy loves you very much. / He just doesn't want to live with us any more".'

The words pinned down a feeling I couldn't shake off. I had to let him go. I had to write about him, in a way that made him feel robust and real, and let myself come through, on my own, spinning by myself, on the other side.

'I Trawl the Megahertz' also told me how unsettling it could be to explore the story of my life. The process, the woman said, could be 'stranger than songs or fiction'. But a song, in all its precision, could also help us confront and challenge ideas of who we were, offering us enlightening new trails to explore.

Just after midnight one night in summer 2021, as lockdowns were finally easing, composer Hannah Peel played 'I Trawl the Megahertz' in full on her Radio 3 *Night Tracks* programme. It felt like a sign. I woke up realising I wanted to speak to Paddy and emailed his manager not long after I had finished my breakfast – but I knew this was unlikely, because since 2006, Paddy had been suffering from Ménière's Disease, a condition which involves hearing loss, vertigo and tinnitus, affecting his ability to play music and even sometimes to speak with other people. The next day, out shopping with my son, I miss a call from a landline phone number with a code I don't recognise. I think nothing of it – a sales call, maybe, or spam – until later I plug my iPhone into the socket in the car. The answering service plays automatically, and once again, Paddy McAloon emerges, to my surprise, from the speakers.

We speak a few days later: Paddy's voice is gentle, quiet, rippling like circles of warm water. He tells me how he started putting the track together on his Atari computer in the late nineties, a machine he's used since the eighties and still uses when he composes today. 'I had been ill, and then my wife and I had just had our first daughter. There was a sort of change where you're not the centre of things any more, and your sleep patterns are a bit disrupted. You might think I could just go out and get a Miles Davis record or get something that doesn't have much vocal information, that has a nice mood going for it – but I wanted to listen to something that I had made myself.'

His inspiration was a book he found at the Windows record shop in Newcastle, called *Boulez on Music Today*. 'All I knew was he was a classical composer, I knew he was avant-garde, I didn't know any more than that. I started to get interested in these guys who had taken music to bits and were trying to build it in a different fashion, even though I wasn't really conversant with how music was built in the first place.' Paddy isn't classically trained, he points out. 'You know, with all the keys and how the tonal system works. I was just fascinated that other people had another take on it – that just fired my imagination.'

Into this, he stirred his interest in a book he liked at the time, Elizabeth Smart's *By Grand Central Station I Sat Down and Wept* ('it was all heightened language, and I liked it, even if, you know, even if I've grown out of it a bit, shall we say'). He was also inspired by Orson Welles' *F for Fake* ('where he'd discovered a way to make a film where he does a lot of narration and uses a lot of found footage, and films a few new scenes'), and by the early poetry of T. S. Eliot ('which makes me sound pretentious when I mention it . . . but all of this was feeding into a thing where I felt I'd found something new for myself').

Paddy then talks about how he felt the female character arrive in his mind, 'which feels very presumptuous of me now . . . and I was too shy and a bit nervous to admit that I'd written most of her speech'. He talks about recording the narrator, an American friend-of-a-friend who he's still in touch with, who was a commodities broker. They spoke on the phone earlier this year. 'She trusted me, really. We just met in a hotel room. I heard her on our answer machine, and as soon as I heard her voice, I knew. Oh yeah, yeah, yeah. You're the one.'

The line 'Daddy loves you very much, he just doesn't want to live with us any more' wasn't fabricated, but taken from a chat show. 'The more I played that back, it kind of struck me as musical, that phrase.' He talks about how words have melodies and rhythms of their own. 'The musicality of any conversation or any sound played back . . . you must know from your tape recordings when you hear them . . . [take] the cadence of my voice on an absolutely boring sentence, play it back five times and go, "I'm hearing the intervals in that and I'm hearing the musicality of it."' He was trying to make his words play like music, he explains, in and of themselves. I realise that this is what I've been doing with my book: trying to make my words rise and fall, fit into a pattern of leaps and twists and resolutions, to give my story its verses, its bridges, its choruses, its coda.

I wonder if I am going mad feeling Paddy's story tally with mine, but then I think about how his song has given me such pleasure and release; how its narrator spoke to me at two very different times in my life; how his song has brought me here, to this conversation, this profound moment of connection, and how encounters like these are the highlights of my professional life. Paddy says he still isn't sure what age the narrator of 'I Trawl the Megahertz' is, though; I love that some of the track is still a mystery to him. 'It feels like it's either a young person, or it's the memories of someone remembering being young and having those feelings.' Perhaps it's both of them — a person's life bouncing back to them in the echo.

He was forty-two to forty-three when he wrote the album, he adds, and asks me how old I am writing this book. He laughs when I tell him the answer — it's exactly the same. Then he spears the moment: 'I think at the heart of all of these things — it's a melancholy thought, but loss is always there. At forty-two, forty-three, you've done the thing that you're supposed to do . . . but you've never really thought about what you do when you get older. For a musician, you still think your songs are valid, but the marketplace changes and there are younger people forever coming in to fulfil the role that you had for a long time. Other people have other versions of that.' You're trying to work out who you are, I say, now your mortality is truly kicking in. 'Yes. And you suddenly realise, oh, *this* is who you are.'

He tells me who he thought he was then, at forty-two, forty-three, from the perspective of someone who is now sixty-four. 'At that age, you've been defined by the records you've made, by the people you know, your parents, your siblings, your friends, but also people you maybe didn't give enough time to, because you were too busy thinking that time was either infinite, or you had enough time to start again.' Back then, he started to see his life behind him in snapshots, he said, and craved melodies to tie the tiny pieces of himself together. The narrator's time in the bar in Paris was influenced by a trip he had taken with an old girlfriend. The bit about someone not speaking the language was about being a baby. 'It's also a metaphor for being on your own until someone shows you what you're doing. I think that's what it is.' He laughs shyly. 'I'm hopefully not spoiling it for you.'

I tell him that I also loved the line about the shoelace, and about the first song I loved after my dad died, about all the songs that followed after. I tell him about first hearing his music by the tills at a supermarket in my home town, feeling my mouth run away with itself, my heart fully split open. He gets it. 'I'm working in my dad's garage as a petrol attendant,' he says. 'I've gone in the house at lunchtime and I'm putting on a pair of trainers or something like that, and I'm bending down and tying my lace, and I hear "Good Times" for the very first time, by Chic. And I just thought, "Ah, that's a record. That's what you call a record," and it's never left me. I can see myself, I can see the shoes, I can see the old crappy radio, so I'm just the same as you. Lots of people are.'

*

I listen to 'I Trawl the Megahertz' again a few weeks after talking to Paddy, and I realise suddenly, with clarity, that the resonances in this song aren't really about me longing for my father. It is about me longing for music, and how songs carry different iterations of me through different times in my life. Words can't do this alone. Songs can capture my thoughts at different moments, say, on a September evening in the rain, just past eight, as my husband is downstairs doing the dishes and listening to a jazz record – it's John Coltrane's 'My Favourite Things'. I can hear it, travelling through the rooms and accompanying our now-seven-year-old's sleep after a busy day in juniors, but also taking me to our old flat in Stoke Newington, opposite the Shakespeare pub, not long before we married, as we were chaotically planning our day, and to car journeys to Wales as we tried to find somewhere new to live. Images can't capture the nuances that a song can either. They can catch the glow in the eyes of a person, or the tiredness or the lines that are adding detail to a face; they can capture a changing body, but not often the intricacies or depths of a changing mind.

But music carries that mind. It sets off sequences of neural connections that began forming before we were babies, that can be reignited in seconds, that last almost until the moment we die. It can shoot a person into the past – to many pasts – while holding them tightly in the present. It fosters love. It makes us want to dance wildly with strangers. It makes so many of us want to speak and move and write and sing. It makes us want to articulate its majesty, quietly, loudly, with variety.

It also stops us forgetting, and I don't want to forget. And I can't forget music - because music never forgets us.

It also takes me to a front porch I still visit today, to see my mam, stepdad and the rest of my growing family, to where the sun often comes out, where bushes are often dark-pink and purple with summer flowers. The terrazzo tiles don't sparkle as brightly as they used to, but as I laughingly think every time, neither do I. Other memories have looped around that scene through the years, though – melodies beginning and ending, harmonies clashing and resolving – creating new rhythms in our lives. Songs make us remember all those details of who we have been and where we have been. We live with them and within them.

They allow us to rewind and pause for a moment, like nothing else does. Then we press play.

Secret Track

The day that I finish my book, I call my mother. I haven't told her the full extent of what I am writing about. I haven't shown anyone, not even my husband, or my best friends, my first draft. I want to share my music, and my stories, so much, but sometimes they still feel too personal. But now it's done, I suddenly have the urge to speak to her.

My mam's name is Alison. Dad's was Roy (yes, he shared my surname, so he was a Welsh cowboy). I realise I haven't asked her what music Dad liked for any of these chapters. I know the book isn't just about him and it isn't just about me. But I have never had this conversation with her specifically, and I want to let him out, let him go, let his music fly free.

We talk after she has come home from choir. I feel nervous asking her, and she sounds nervous answering. 'I remember him loving "Bird on the Wire",' she says, quickly but warmly. I remember Dad's copy of *Songs from a Room*, on which this song was the first track, the shiny white sleeve, and the picture of Marianne Ihlen, his girlfriend, wrapped in a towel sitting at her boyfriend's typewriter, on the back. This came out in 1969, the year Mam and Dad got together. Footage from the moon landings was playing on a TV in their teacher training college, Mam says, around the time she first saw him.

Dad used to play Leonard Cohen a lot, she continues. Often, he'd sit in the corner on his own to listen to it through his headphones. He bought *Songs of Love and*

Hate a few years later: on its cover is a black-and-white photo of Leonard, not looking entirely himself. I stole this album from home when I was eighteen, thinking the picture looked a bit like my father, the darkness of his hair bleeding into the background. I framed it a few years after that. It's lived in every house with me ever since, and still looks down at me now from the messy record shelves in my office.

But when I listen to it, I don't think of Dad. I think of how cataclysmic an experience it was first hearing 'Avalanche', and how I like to play it when it's dark, in the car, looking at the road ahead with the lights on full beam. I think of how I learned 'Famous Blue Raincoat' on the guitar in my early twenties, sitting on an old Ikea sofa in my dressing gown, trying to be sincerely L. Cohen. When I think of the rain falling on last year's man, I see a Canadian poet, not a Welsh father.

'What else did he like? He liked The Beatles. Bob Dylan. Billy Joel. ABBA. The Bee Gees. Lots of stuff from the charts. Disco. Oh, and Bruce Springsteen.' I never knew he liked Bruce Springsteen. This was before *Born in the USA* – was it *The River*? *Darkness on the Edge of Town*? *Born to Run*? *Nebraska*? I'd never know. It was OK. 'And Irish country and folk things, like Clannad. He had a tape of all that music.' I remember being obsessed with 'Harry's Game' when I was about fourteen, copied off that compilation, but I didn't clock it was his. Would you listen along with him? 'Some of it, yes. A lot. I'd tolerate it sometimes!' The music bristles in our laughter.

Mam liked Neil Diamond, and classical music – operas, oratorios, musical theatre – as she would do for the rest of her life. Dad would play that for her too. She's also enjoyed this music ever since with my stepfather, going to concerts and shows, sharing that joy with another person she loves.

'But obviously when I think of your dad most,' she says, her voice sounding very young, 'I think of Ralph McTell.'

From when they were first going out, Mam and Dad both loved Ralph McTell. On one of their first dates, they went to see him in Bindles in Barry Island (I look it up online: it was a small concrete ballroom, raised on high modernist pillars, demolished in 1981). It was on a Friday night, Mam says, after she was on a probationary course in her first year. I love these shadows of the younger her. Later, I'd watch Ralph's programmes for children on TV, *Alphabet Zoo* and *Tickle on the Tum*, his shows inspired by the folk songs for kids by Woody Guthrie. I assume I watched them sometimes with my father.

Before I left home, Mam stuck the lyrics to one of Ralph's songs, 'An Irish Blessing', from his 1995 album *Sand in Your Shoes*, to our fridge. I was seventeen, dressing like one of the Velvet Underground, thinking she was being daftly sentimental. Now I am older, I understand her going to one of her favourite musicians for comfort and advice. 'How my life is changing now,' it read. 'My young ones start to leave their home/ I wish that their uncertain road/ Was one that I could tread with them.' She must have wanted Jon and me to see it when we went to drain the fridge of food and beer, to understand the love of an artist who had meant so much to her and Dad, to carry his words and hers with us.

I've since interviewed Ralph McTell twice, most recently in 2019, with Tony Visconti in the Groucho Club. Visconti's sharp glasses and tight trousers made him look like a new wave elder. Ralph, his old friend, was wearing double denim and earrings. The first thing Ralph asked made me love him even more. 'How is your mum?' He recalled me speaking to him in 2011 straightaway, in Newport, before a gig: I'd taken along my mother to meet him. I told him about my father's love for him, as did she. She squealed with excitement in the corridor straight after. I loved imagining her all those years ago, seeing her just like I used to be – although in many ways, that's who I still am.

I realised Mam still had more stories to tell me, about her life as much as my father's. There were more songs I had to hear from her and from other family and friends, so many combinations of notes and ideas that revealed other sides of people I knew.

I think now of Ralph telling me how he loved 'the humility of music' on that evening in Newport, how he adored its unpretentiousness and modesty despite its power and magnitude. It is a humble thing, really, always there, hovering in the wings or the airwaves, waiting to be let out, waiting to surprise us. Ralph also reminded me that it will outlive us all: 'Music has been there before you, and it will be there after you.'

I like this idea. We just pick up on its vibrations for a while – its dynamism, its subtleties, its allure – as we come and go in its wake. Off you go, my love, shimmering and singing to yourself, to the universe.

Acknowledgements

So many thanks and so much love to everyone that follows:

Mrs Gill at Penyrheol Comp for telling me I could write a book one day. It only took me twenty-eight years, Janet, but I did it!

The Word Magazine (RIP) massive. I wouldn't be here without you.

Ellie Levenson and Alex Farebrother-Naylor, and the book we made together in 2015, *Pop! For Kids*. It lit a touchpaper.

Colin Grant and Caitlin Davies: your mentoring at your brilliant Arvon week helped my proposal come to life.

Stuart Evers, Luce Brett, Luke Turner, Kathryn Williams and Kat Lister – writers and confidantes – for your anxiety-soothing advice, guidance and friendship.

Georgia Moody, Tess Davidson and Barney Rowntree at Reduced Listening for your enthusiasm and help with research for our 2021 BBC Radio 4 series, *A Life in Music*.

Every expert, writer and friend I interviewed for the book: I'm sorry I couldn't have space for all of you. A special thanks to Catherine Loveday for casting an educated eye over my scientific summaries.

The editors for whom I wrote pieces that provided inspirations for this book: Michael Hann, David Hepworth, Laura Snapes and John Doran, among others. Thanks for paying for my self-directed therapy sessions.

Lee, Ellie, Maura, Katie, Lucinda, Tom and everyone at Orion/White Rabbit for your boundless encouragement. Kasimiira and Leighanne at Atelier PR for being absolute powerhouses. And Debbie Holmes – thanks so much for designing such a fantastic cover.

Lisa Baker at Aitken Alexander for your clear head, your dirty laugh, and for giving me confidence.

My friends, including those mentioned in this book and others whose rhythms nevertheless pulse in its pages: I have a song for almost every one of you. I love all of them.

My family: Mam, Dad R, Jon, Dad P, James, the whole extended gang. There is so much music through which your stories sing to me. You sing them so beautifully.

To Dan, for the laughter, the constant, unwavering support, the badgering me that, yes, Jude, you can do this, the unexpected, brilliant copy-edit, your amazing skills as a Dad, your unceasing love.

To E for the music you bring into my world every day, every hour, every moment. Your Grandpa would have been so very proud of you. Keep the music in your heart, my love, and keep playing it loud.